The Outdoor
Build-It Book

The Outdoor Build-It Book

JACK KRAMER

CHARLES SCRIBNER'S SONS / New York

Acknowledgments

I wish to express my thanks to the following companies for their cooperation and for the use of their photos in the making of this book:

American Plywood Association
Western Wood Products
California Redwood Association
General Electric Company
American Canvas Institute
Tile Council of America
Portland Cement Association

11-12-85

Library of Congress Cataloging in Publication Data
Kramer, Jack, 1927-
  The outdoor garden build-it book.
    1. Garden structures—Design and construction.
I. Title.
TH4962.K7   690.8'9   76-52761
ISBN 0-684-14762-9
ISBN 0-684-15039-5 pbk.

1. Frontispiece: A formal patio using concrete floors and lovely lattice fences creates a striking scene. (*Photo by Max Eckert, Perkins, Designer*)

Contents

The Outdoor
Build-It Book

2. Wood is a versatile outdoor building material; here it is used for a patio deck at varying levels and also for fencing. The sandbox play area is also made from wood. (*Photo courtesy American Plywood Association*)

1. Materials

LUMBER

Lumber is the most important material in building construction and is the workhorse of the garden. It is used for fences, walls, retaining walls, planter beds (permanent or modular), lath houses, storage sheds, tool sheds, overhangs for patios, furniture, bird feeders, and so on. It is the one material you will be using constantly if you do any kind of garden construction.

Lumber is an easy material to use and both men and women (even those not handy with tools) generally can work with lumber. But there are many grades of lumber, many kinds of lumber, and it is just as important to know these facts about the material so you can buy lumber cheaply and buy the right lumber for a job as it is to know how to put things together.

There are many kinds of lumber—Douglas fir, pine, redwood, for example—and many grades, such as Construction Grade, All Heartwood, and so on. (We list all of these woods and their uses later.) For now, remember that all lumber, no matter what grade, is not true to size. When you buy a 2-by-4-inch piece of lumber you do not get 2 by 4. The actual dimension may be $1\frac{9}{16}$ by $3\frac{9}{16}$ if it is unseasoned (not dried) and $1\frac{1}{2}$ by $3\frac{1}{2}$ if it is seasoned (dried).

Redwood is generally the best lumber to use outdoors because it is a weather-resistant wood. This means it has natural chemicals within it that thwart termites and fungus. It can be used natural or with a protective coating. Left to weather it turns a beautiful silvery color and lasts for about seven years. If stained or painted it lasts longer. Redwood is fine grained, blends well with outdoor surroundings, and when plentiful, is inexpensive.

Cedar is another good wood, but it is usually difficult to find and costly. It has a handsome appearance and like redwood resists decay and weather. Douglas fir, less aesthetically pleasing than redwood or cedar, has a tendency to rot when exposed to severe weather conditions unless it has a protective coating or paint. (Many preparations may be found at hardware stores.)

GRADES OF LUMBER. Lumber comes in grades such as Select, Clear, All Heart, Construction Heart, Construction Common, and Merchantable. Generally, your lumber dealer will advise you what you need for a particular structure, but I always believe in knowing something about what I am buying, not only to get my money's worth, but also to work better with the material I am using. Here is how lumber is graded:

Clear Heart Redwood. A superior (and expensive) all-heartwood grade for architectural use. Highly decay resistant and free of knots. Can be used for posts.

Select Heart. All-heartwood grade that has some small knots and torn grain. High strength and durability.

Construction Heart. A good commercial decay-resistant grade with some large knots.

A-Grade. May contain cream-colored sapwood. Is less resistant to decay than all-heartwood grades. Free of imperfections.

Construction Common (rough lumber) . Similar to Construction Heart except that sapwood and medium stain are permitted and it has tight knots.

Merchantable. Contains more knots and defects (loose knots and knotholes in some areas) than the higher sapwood grades. Economical.

Kiln-dried lumber is not required for garden structures although it is sometimes used for posts or ornamental members; air-seasoned lumber generally performs well. However, lumber that is too green (has too much

*Garden Grade Lumbers

3. For fences, wood can take many shapes and forms; this handsome fence uses posts and strips. The members have been painted for eye appeal. (*Photo by Ken Molino*)

moisture) is likely to shrink and pull loose from fastenings after a time.

The various grades of lumber have many surface textures. Clear Heartwood, A-Grade, and Common Grade generally are surfaced on both sides to a smooth finish. Select Heart or Construction Heart may come from the mill with a rough surface. These grades are satisfactory for most garden construction but difficult to paint. Saw-texture lumber is not the same as rough lumber; it is more expensive and has a handsome resawn quality.

Even within the specific grades of lumber there are variations, so try to select lumber personally rather than to have it selected for you. That way, you can select boards with fewer defects. Also, occasionally lumber will be warped or not square. This is allowable in the lumber trade but can wreak havoc for the amateur carpenter.

DIMENSIONS OF LUMBER. As mentioned earlier, the actual size of a piece of wood is not what the dimensions say, so for easy reference, the following is a table of standard dimensions (in inches) for unseasoned boards and kiln-dried lumber:

UNSEASONED BOARDS
(generally used for outdoor work)

SIZE TO ORDER	ACTUAL SIZE
1 by 3	$^{25}\!/_{32}$ by $2^{9}\!/_{16}$
1 by 4	$^{25}\!/_{32}$ by $3^{9}\!/_{16}$
1 by 6	$^{25}\!/_{32}$ by $5^{5}\!/_{8}$
1 by 8	$^{25}\!/_{32}$ by $7\frac{1}{4}$
2 by 3	$1^{9}\!/_{16}$ by $2^{9}\!/_{16}$
2 by 4	$1^{9}\!/_{16}$ by $3^{9}\!/_{16}$
2 by 6	$1^{9}\!/_{16}$ by $5^{5}\!/_{8}$
2 by 8	$1^{9}\!/_{16}$ by $7\frac{1}{2}$
2 by 10	$1^{9}\!/_{16}$ by $9\frac{1}{2}$

KILN-DRIED LUMBER

SIZE TO ORDER	ACTUAL SIZE
1 by 4	$\frac{3}{4}$ by $3\frac{1}{2}$
1 by 6	$\frac{3}{4}$ by $5\frac{1}{2}$
1 by 8	$\frac{3}{4}$ by $7\frac{1}{4}$
2 by 4	$1\frac{1}{2}$ by $3\frac{1}{2}$
2 by 6	$1\frac{1}{2}$ by $5\frac{1}{2}$
2 by 8	$1\frac{1}{2}$ by $7\frac{1}{4}$

DETERMINING HOW MUCH LUMBER. Stock-sized lumber is based and priced on even-inch dimensions; for example, a 2-by-4-inch board comes in 8-, 10-, or 12-foot lengths. Bear this in mind when ordering.

4. Wood is used throughout this patio garden—for decking, fencing, and as an overhang—and the results are charming. Some of the wood is natural; other pieces have been painted for contrast. (*Photo courtesy California Redwood Association*)

Trying to determine how much lumber you need for a fence or for a garden bench can be complicated. However, all lumber dealers will help you if you have the exact dimensions of what you are making. You can even get lumber cut to exact size but this, of course, will be more expensive than cutting the lumber yourself; extra labor is involved. So, if you have a power saw, buy lumber and do the cutting. If you do not have a saw, you will simply have to pay the additional cost.

By the way, lumber is delivered tail gate, that is, dumped in one specific spot; then it is up to you to move it to the building area. It makes

5. For benches and for the island deck, construction-grade redwood has been used; wood is a perfect foil for the concrete patio. (*Photo courtesy California Redwood Association*)

good sense to tell the delivery man *exactly* where you want the lumber. Get it dumped as close to the building site as possible to save you from carrying it around.

CONCRETE AND DECORATIVE BLOCK

Concrete blocks are another good outdoor building material with many uses. You can make walls and planters with them, and you can use them for pavings, too. You can buy blocks with color (green or tan) cast in them, or use blocks in their natural gray color and waterproof them with a silicone liquid. There are patterned and textured blocks in a great variety of designs—the most common concrete block is 16 inches long, 8 inches high, and 8 inches wide. Foot-square and 4-inch blocks are also offered, and blocks are also available in brick shapes, solid rather than hollow. In addition to the standard blocks there are half, corner, double-corner, bullnose, and channel blocks for wall building.

MIXING CONCRETE. Concrete is a plastic material composed of gravel and sand, held together by cement and water. If you have brick walls or walks, floors, or whatever, you will be using concrete in one way or another. You can buy ingredients and make your own concrete or have concrete (already mixed) delivered to the site. For small jobs in garden construction—walks, setting posts—simply use dry-mix sacks of concrete. All you have to do is add water. For large expanses of concrete such as a patio floor or a long walk, buy concrete ready-mixed delivered to the site.

6. Concrete aggregate is the choice of material for this patio; wood again is used for fencing; the result is totally charming. (*Photo courtesy* **Western Wood Products Association**)

7. Here, a solid concrete patio area is used around the pool; it is durable, easy to clean, and inexpensive. (*Photo courtesy National Cotton Council*)

To estimate the amount of concrete you will need for a project, measure the length and breadth in feet and the thickness in a fraction of a foot. Multiply the three figures together to determine just how many cubic feet of concrete are needed. For example, if a walk is 3 feet by 20 feet with a thickness of 4 inches (⅓ of a foot), you would need about 20 cubic feet or about ⅘ of a cubic yard of concrete.

You can mix concrete in a wheelbarrow by hand, or rent a power or hand-operated concrete mixer. This expedites matters greatly and the machine is not difficult to use. Whatever the mixing method you decide to use, the ingredients of concrete are Portland cement, fine aggregate (stones), coarse aggregate (larger stones), and water. Portland cement is sold in sacks of 1 cubic foot. Coarse aggregate consists of well-ground

8. Concrete block is frequently used for patios; it is easy to install and creates interest for floors. (*Photo courtesy National Concrete Masonry Association*)

gravel or crushed rock; fine aggregate is made of stones less than ¼ inch in diameter. The amount of water used per sack of cement determines the strength of the concrete.

Generally, for most concrete work you should use 6 gallons of water for each commercial sack of cement. To mix the concrete put 2 shovelfuls of sand into the wheelbarrow and add 1 shovelful of cement. Mix thoroughly, add 3 shovelfuls of gravel, and mix again. Add water from a garden hose, a little at a time, mixing as you go. Continue mixing all ingredients until they are well combined and of the desired stiffness. If you have added too much water, add some more sand, gravel, and cement. If the mixture is too thick, add more water. Whether using a hand or power mixer, follow the same procedure.

9. Brick is the choice for this patio; this material is always handsome and can be used in many patterns. It is easy to install, durable, and blends well with outdoor greenery. (*Photo courtesy Western Wood Products Association*)

BRICK

The beauty of brick as a natural material is well known; it harmonizes beautifully with most outdoor situations. Whether in a straight, L-shaped, or serpentine wall, or for a patio floor, brick has charm and lasts for years.

The average brick wall is 8 or more inches thick (two bricks wide) and requires steel reinforcing rods in mortar joints at frequent intervals. Very large walls will have to be reinforced about every 12 feet with a brick pier or pilaster. This type of construction usually requires the help of a professional mason, unless you are very handy with tools. For those who want to do their own brick wall, you will need a pointed trowel for buttering mortar, a broad-bladed cold chisel, a hammer, a level, and a carpenter's square.

Common brick is laid damp; to hold the mortar you need a mortar board, a piece of wood—say the top of an orange crate. Scoop the mortar (enough for only a few bricks) from the board with the trowel, and spread it over the top course of bricks. Put each brick in place, trim away mortar to butter the end of the next brick, and continue until more mortar is needed. Set bricks into perfect alignment by tapping them into place gently. Build the ends or corners first because this will make it easier to set the next bricks in line. Use a nylon line as a guide to keep bricks in alignment as you install them. Anchor the ends of the line into mortar joints. Before the mortar sets, trim away loose bits and smooth off all joints.

Mortar for bricklaying is a mixture of 2 parts Portland cement, 1 part fireclay or lime, and 9 parts garden sand. Supplies are sold at hardware and lumber stores.

TOOLS AND HARDWARE NEEDED

You do not need too many tools for garden construction: a hammer, saws, drill, and tape measure are necessary, and it is wise to buy the very best you can afford. Cheap tools are invariably worthless and last a short time. Also, keep tools out of weather in a storage area where you can always get hold of them. An old-fashioned carpenter's apron is also a convenience. (Lumber dealers give this away as a premium; or buy one—it's worth the price.) You can of course have other carpentry tools, but essentially those listed here are all you'll need to do most wood construction.

For setting concrete or laying tile and brick, other tools will be needed; these are covered in the chapters that follow.

2. Patios

No matter where you live, if you have any outdoor space, a patio is a desirable addition to the property. It is a delightful place in which to spend time away from a busy world. Patios can be expensive if done by professionals or reasonable if you do most of the work yourself. You do not have to be very handy with tools to install a modest patio.

The idea of making your own patio may frighten you. Don't let it. Laying a brick patio on sand, for example, is a simple job that takes more patience than skill. Even using ready-mixed poured concrete isn't that difficult (the various techniques are explained later). With concrete delivered to the site, try to have a few friends on hand to help you with your project. One of the most difficult parts of installing a patio floor used to be building the wooden forms to contain the concrete until it sets. Now you can rent metal forms, which work better than wooden ones, at rent-it shops.

The patio can be a simple exposed area with a few plants adjacent to the living or dining room or a partially enclosed area (see chapter 3). If you enjoy outdoor cookery and dining, a patio can be enclosed—almost an outdoor room. This provides additional living space.

SIZE AND LOCATION

Sun, rain, and wind must be considered before you decide where the patio will be. The patio that is in sun most of the day will be too warm for your personal use by day. And a patio that is in constant wind is not a comfortable place for either plants or people. Screens, fences, canopies, and trees and shrubs can somewhat modify the elements but never totally eliminate wind.

14

10.Interest and charm are the keynotes of this small patio. The elevated design gives it drama and at the same time provides a viewing place. (*Photo by Ken Molino*)

A south patio basks in sun; in chilly climates it can be a blessing, but in arid regions it becomes an annoyance. A west patio is ideal in the morning, but during the day it may become uncomfortably warm. A patio that faces east is an ideal area; there is morning sun, but in the afternoon it is cool and shady. Northern exposures need not be neglected. Many plants thrive in shade.

Don't make the outdoor area so large that it becomes a bleak expanse of gray concrete. These patios are more depressing than cheerful.

PATIO PAVINGS

Materials for outdoor floors include brick, tile, concrete, paving blocks, fieldstone, and flagstone. Others such as loose-fill materials, gravel chips, fir bark, cinders, plastic stones, lavarock, dolomite, and crushed brick are temporary and will have to be replaced yearly. So is indoor-out-

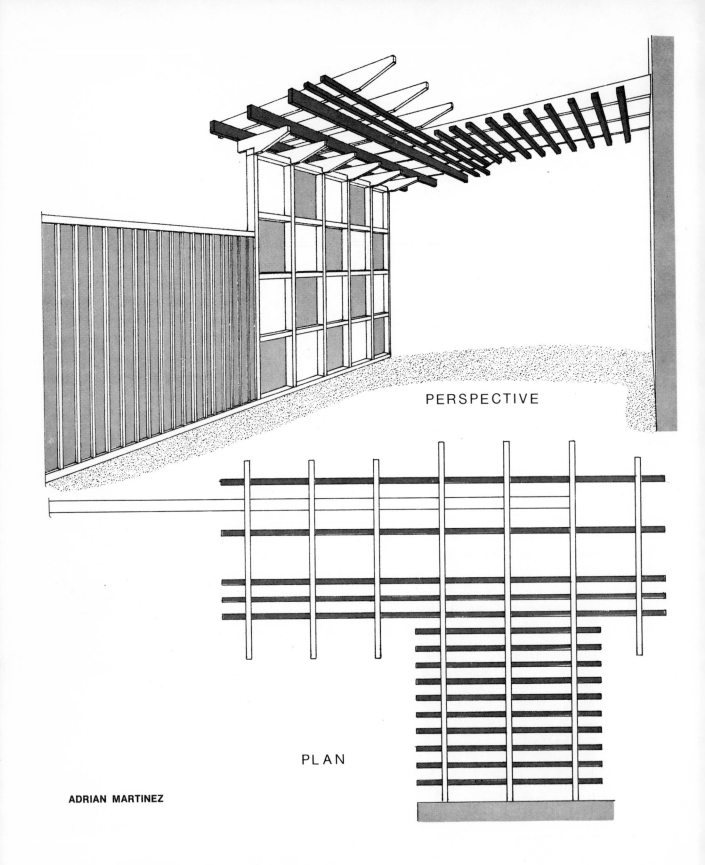

PERSPECTIVE

PLAN

ADRIAN MARTINEZ

Patio Enclosure

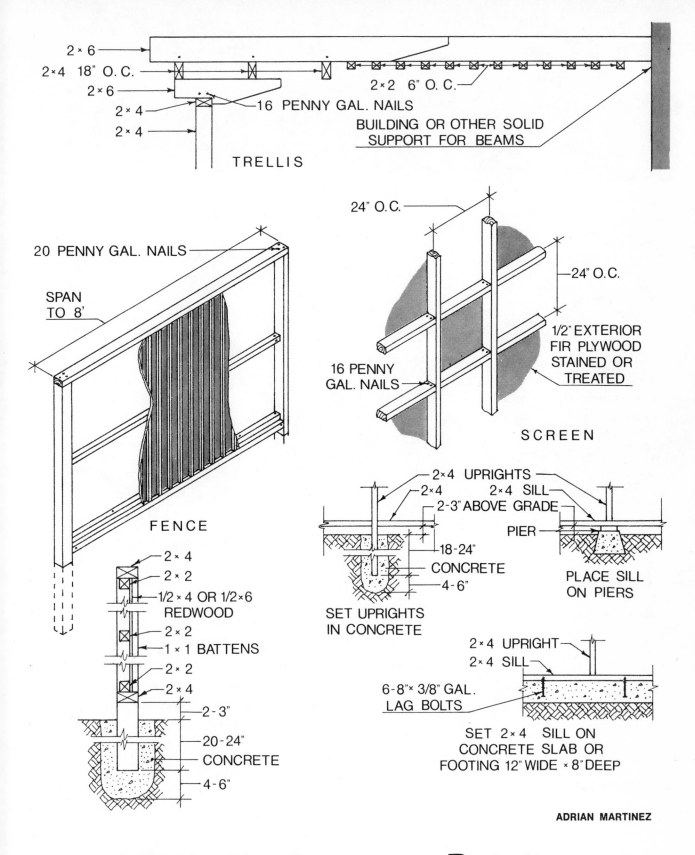

2 × 6

2 × 4 18" O.C.

2 × 6

2 × 4

2 × 4

16 PENNY GAL. NAILS

2 × 2 6" O.C.

BUILDING OR OTHER SOLID
SUPPORT FOR BEAMS

TRELLIS

24" O.C.

24" O.C.

20 PENNY GAL. NAILS

SPAN
TO 8'

16 PENNY
GAL. NAILS

1/2" EXTERIOR
FIR PLYWOOD
STAINED OR
TREATED

SCREEN

FENCE

2 × 4

2 × 2

1/2 × 4 OR 1/2 × 6
REDWOOD

2 × 2

1 × 1 BATTENS

2 × 2

2 × 4

2 - 3"

20 - 24"

CONCRETE

4 - 6"

2 × 4 UPRIGHTS

2 × 4

2 - 3" ABOVE GRADE

2 × 4 SILL

PIER

18 - 24"

CONCRETE

4 - 6"

SET UPRIGHTS
IN CONCRETE

PLACE SILL
ON PIERS

2 × 4 UPRIGHT

2 × 4 SILL

6 - 8" × 3/8" GAL.
LAG BOLTS

SET 2 × 4 SILL ON
CONCRETE SLAB OR
FOOTING 12" WIDE × 8" DEEP

ADRIAN MARTINEZ

Patio Enclosure   Detail

11. This patio is large so an unusual shape was adopted for eye interest. The two-level design breaks the monotony of a large patio and makes it more handsome. (*Photo courtesy American Canvas Institute*)

door carpeting, which now comes in many colors and designs and in easy-to-install squares.

Because there are so many outdoor floor materials, select one that is in character with the house and choose it for durability and service. A floor that is not comfortable to walk on (gravel) and needs constant cleaning (textured concrete, for example) is a bad choice. And, finally, in selecting the patio floor, consider the cost and installation fees.

The following information on paving materials includes the most popular floors—concrete, tile, brick, patio or paving blocks, wood blocks, and round, loose-fill materials—and how to use them. It also touches on less popular but equally attractive floors of flagstone, fieldstone, slate, and all-weather carpeting.

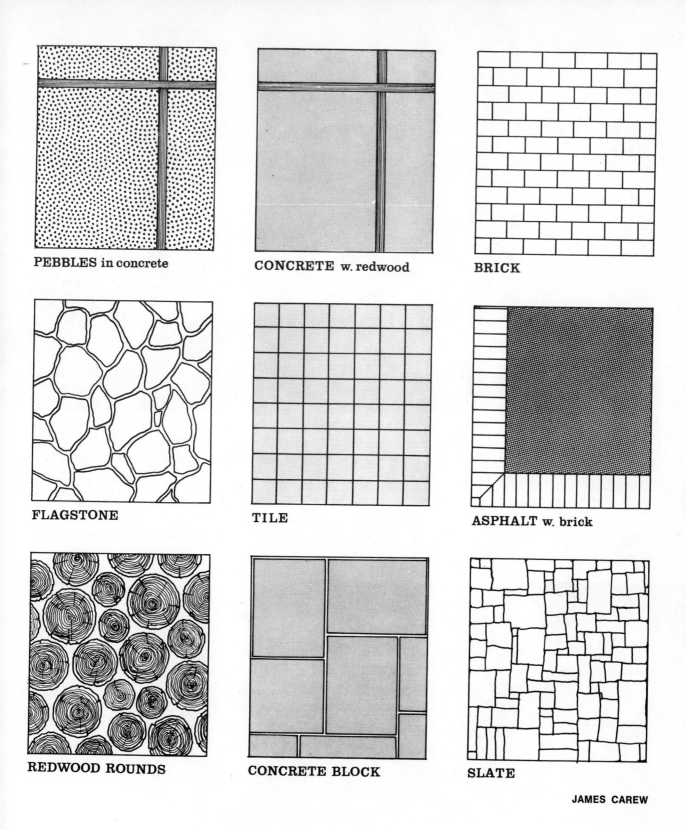

PEBBLES in concrete

CONCRETE w. redwood

BRICK

FLAGSTONE

TILE

ASPHALT w. brick

REDWOOD ROUNDS

CONCRETE BLOCK

SLATE

JAMES CAREW

Patio Pavings

12. Whether a deck or a patio, this elevated wooden area affords a fine outdoor place to relax. The construction is simple and the cost minimal. (*Photo courtesy Leo Woodward Furniture*)

13. A simple inexpensive wooden deck patio is quite pleasing; it affords a retreat close to the house and joins the outdoors with the indoors. (*Photo courtesy Western Wood Products*)

CONCRETE.   Concrete may not be as handsome as some other pavings, but it is a durable, low-cost, and permanent surface. It is easy to clean and a paving contractor can install it completely in a few hours. If you object to the cold feeling of concrete, it can be mixed with color or covered with paint. Or the top layer can be dyed with liquid which seeps deeply into the pores of the concrete. It can also be rough or textured.

An aggregate floor is another idea. It is made of concrete that has small stones on the surface. The textured finish is handsome and blends with plantings and lawns. The uneven texture breaks the monotony of a large area of paving, especially when it is framed with wood grids. The pebbly surface of aggregate concrete also eliminates glare and guarantees sure traction in wet weather. And when this paving collects dirt—as it will—it is easy to wash clean with a strong hosing.

While you can install a small area of concrete yourself, it is best to hire a professional for the large job. However, you can save part of the cost of the floor by having the area ready for him. Outline the patio by setting out 2-by-2-inch stakes with string stretched between them. Dig out and remove all trash from the soil. Set either permanent or temporary header boards in place. Be sure to set headers so the top surface is flush with the grade you want for the concrete. Drive additional stakes at 2-foot intervals along each side of the patio, lined up carefully with the guide string. Nail 10-inch strips of ¼-inch plywood to the insides of the stakes to act as forms for the concrete. Forms can be brushed with oil to make it easier to remove them after the concrete is poured and set.

Wet the soil a few times the day before the concrete is to be poured. The night before, wet it again so it will be damp when the concrete is poured. Soil that is dry takes moisture from the concrete and weakens it.

To build a small patio, rent a portable mixer—ask for a half-bag machine—revolved by a gasoline motor. Put 1 cubic foot of sand and half a sack of cement into the revolving drum. Allow the materials to mix. Then add 1 cubic foot of gravel, and let the drum revolve for a few minutes or until the pebbles are uniformly coated. Now add to the drum about 2 gallons of water, and let the mixture tumble for about 4 minutes. Pour it into a wheelbarrow (rented from the hardware store) and dump the mixture into the forms. Make pavings 3 to 4 inches thick. Smooth out the wet concrete with a wood float tool. Different finishes can be applied for variation.

14. Laying out a patio area with wood boards; string can also be used.

15. Setting up a wood form for concrete paving.

16. Leveling the area; ready for concrete.

17. Smoothing the concrete in place.

The slick, or hard, finish is made by moving a steel trowel over the surface when it is partially hardened. Do the first troweling lightly, just enough to smooth the float texture. Then trowel again with more pressure. This floor is slick and somewhat uninteresting.

The wood float method leaves a floor smooth but not shiny. It is done with the mason's wood trowel (float).

The broom finish gives an interesting texture. It is made by brushing the slightly hardened concrete with a push broom.

18. Leveling the concrete pour.

(*Photos courtesy Portland Cement Association*)

19. Concrete floor and wood louvers create a handsome small patio; the wooden enclosures at the sides provide privacy and make the area intimate. (*Photo courtesy Western Wood Products*)

20. Concrete aggregate and wood combine to provide a lovely patio area. The wood island area is elevated for drama and dimension. (*Photo courtesy Western Wood Products*)

21. Patios need not be large; this is postage-stamp size and still it affords a patio place. (*Photo by Roger Scharmer*)

22. Here a concrete aggregate patio surrounds a lawn and is indeed effective. The combination of gray concrete and green grass is highly pleasing. (*Photo by Ken Molino*)

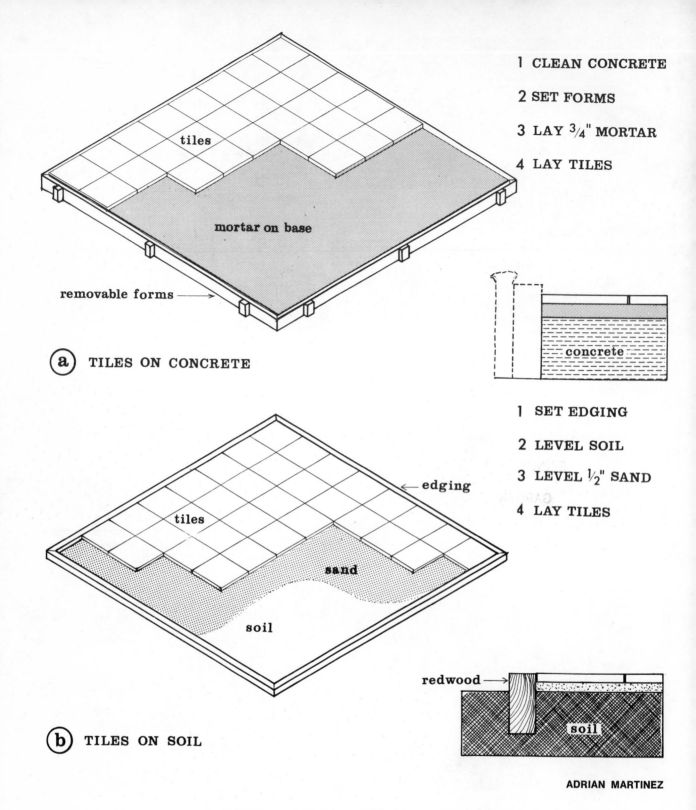

1 CLEAN CONCRETE

2 SET FORMS

3 LAY ¾" MORTAR

4 LAY TILES

tiles

mortar on base

removable forms ⟶

concrete

ⓐ TILES ON CONCRETE

1 SET EDGING

2 LEVEL SOIL

3 LEVEL ½" SAND

4 LAY TILES

tiles

⟵ edging

sand

soil

redwood ⟶

soil

ⓑ TILES ON SOIL

ADRIAN MARTINEZ

How to Set Tile

TILE.   The brown or red color of most tile harmonizes well with green plants. Tile is smoother than brick and easier to clean, and it has a lovely finished look when properly installed. If the patio floor extends into the house, tile is always the decorator's choice.

Outdoor tile is almost always rough-surfaced and usually ¾ inch or ⅞ inch thick. Of the many tiles offered, quarry makes the best patio floor. It is a heavy-duty ceramic material that comes in squares or rectangles or in special shapes. Standard sizes: 3 by 3 inches to 9 by 9 inches. Some have lightly textured surfaces, others fired-in designs. Colors run from off-white to blue green, with red hues the most popular.

Most but not all tiles need a mortar bed to be safe from cracking and it is best to have a professional do the work.

If the soil is flat and stable and you want to try to lay tile on a bed of sand and earth, by all means do so, using the following process. Dig out the soil to about 1 inch below the desired grade and tamp down or roll the earth smooth. Put the outer border in place—rows of tile or header boards—and allow a drainage slope of ⅛ inch per foot. Install a ½-inch bed of sand and level it with a board. Do not use more than a ½-inch bed of sand; tiles may tilt when you step on them. Set the tiles in place starting in a corner and butt them tightly against each other. Tap each one with a wooden block to bed it into the sand firmly.

BRICK.   Brick is a popular paving because it is handsome, easy to install, and lasts a long time. You can set brick in mortar or use the simple method of brick-on-sand. This allows for mistakes; it is easy to take up sections and re-lay them.

Brick comes in a variety of earthy colors, in rough and smooth surfaces, glazed or unglazed. There are many shapes, including hexagons, octagons, fleur-de-lis. And colored brick—green, blue, olive—is also offered now.

Generally, try to choose hard-burned rather than green brick for outdoors. It should be dark red in color rather than salmon color, which indicates an underburned process and is less durable. When you decide on the kind of brick for the floor, be sure the dealer has a sufficient quantity to complete the area. There is usually some dimensional variation and color difference between bricks, so do not complicate your project by not purchasing enough of the same lot.

1 set headers as guide - spread out 2 layers of sand

2 smooth sand with screed

3 position bricks firmly in place

4 level bricks with iron tamp or heavy post

5 sweep sand into cracks

JAMES CAREW

Laying Bricks In Sand

23. A rectangular brick patio with large planter boxes creates this outdoor scene. Note the handsome canvas overhead as a protection from sun. The canvas can be opened or closed depending on weather and the total effect of the patio is charming. (*Photo courtesy American Canvas Institute*)

If you are in a climate where winters are severe specify SW (severe weathering) brick.

It is simple to install a brick-on-sand paving, if you do it in sections—a small piece at a time—rather than try to finish an entire floor in a day.

Brick can be laid in an incredible number of patterns—herringbone, basketweave, and running bond, for example. Or brick can also be combined with other materials—squares of grass or cinders—in endless designs. The herringbone pattern is handsome for large areas; use running bond or a basketweave design for smaller areas. Or the area can be a grid pattern of redwood with bricks.

To cut or trim bricks cut a groove along one side of the brick with a cold chisel and then give it a final severing blow. Smooth uneven bricks by rubbing the edges with another brick.

Install brick on sand as follows: Grade the soil with a board and

24. Brick always makes a handsome paving and is used in a triangular design here to coordinate with the garden. (*Photo by Ken Molino*)

25. Used brick, rustic in character, is the patio paving in an informal garden. (*Photo by Roger Scharmer*)

26. Patios need not be rectangular; this unusually shaped patio is quite handsome bordered with a small brick parapet wall. (*Photo by Ken Molino*)

tamp it down thoroughly. Get rid of lumpy clay and debris. Slope the floor away from the house—1 inch to 6 feet of paving—to allow for drainage. Put in a 2-to-3-inch bed of sand that is absolutely level. Set the bricks as close together as possible and check each row with a level as you go. Then dust sand into the cracks.

For edgings, use 2-by-4-inch wooden header strips held firmly in place with stakes, or a border of bricks set in concrete.

Brick can also be set in mortar, but this is usually a job for a professional bricklayer.

27. Close-up of concrete block patio installation. (*Photo courtesy Portland Cement Association*)

PATIO BLOCKS. Thick patio blocks or pavers are made of concrete that has been vibrated under pressure. They are made in several shapes—hexagonal, round, and random—in several colors. You can install pavers directly on a sand base so that they are free to move and are not rigid in place. This almost eliminates the cracking that can occur in a poured concrete floor.

To install patio pavers, mark the boundaries with string and stakes and remove about 2 inches of soil. Dampen the soil and then add sand and tamp it down. Be sure the sand base is level and establish a slope away from the house for drainage. Place a sheet of polyethylene over the sand to prevent weeds or grass from growing up between the blocks. Start in a corner to install blocks and be sure each block is fitted into place absolutely level.

28. Here concrete blocks are used for patio paving. (*Photo courtesy Portland Cement Association*)

29. A random concrete block installation. (*Photo courtesy Portland Cement Association*)

30. Large aggregate in concrete makes a handsome patio floor. (*Photo courtesy Portland Cement Association*)

31. Concrete pads are used as paving material for this patio/swimming pool area. Concrete is inexpensive and easy to install, and the bright area complements the grass expanse. (*Photo by Ken Molino*)

32. For the indoor patio and for the street, concrete is used here as the paving material. It is clean, effective, and blends well with its surroundings. (*Photo courtesy Western Wood Products*)

33. Random pieces of concrete used as patio paving. (*Photo courtesy Portland Cement Association*)

34. A concrete aggregate patio floor with wood spacers is the paving for this small area. (*Photo by Matthew Barr*)

WOOD BLOCKS AND ROUNDS. Blocks and rounds of wood look natural in a woodland setting. The rounds, about 4 inches thick, are cut from trunks of redwood, cedar, or cypress and can be placed in a random fashion on a sand base. Square blocks are pieces of lumber or cut-up railroad ties. Even coated with preservatives, wood paving only lasts about five years. It is likely to crack in intense sun or split in severe frosts. Yet wood rounds and pieces of railroad ties can easily be removed and replaced with other paving material when the time comes.

Redwood rounds come in lengths from 6 to 36 inches and are easily set in place over sand. Grade the soil and put in a 2-inch sand base and place the rounds in a random pattern; fill in between them with soil or crushed gravel.

To install wood blocks, dig out the soil to a depth of 1 inch greater than the thickness of the blocks. Tamp down the ground and fill with a 1-inch sand base. Place the blocks in the desired pattern. Fill spaces between them with sand.

LOOSE-FILL MATERIALS.

Loose-fill flooring is inexpensive and easily installed in a few hours. It can be attractive too. There are many materials for flooring.

Wood or fir bark chips are popular because they are easily put into place and are attractive. They come in small-, medium-, or large-grade sizes. The large-grade size is the most satisfactory and lasts for about two years. The brownish red color adds warmth to an area. Fir bark chips are sold under different trade names by the bag, usually containing 40 cubic feet.

Lavarock consists of pieces of porous stone; it is available under different trade names and in different colors. It is difficult to walk on and in time wears away; however, it is a simple, inexpensive covering that can be replaced with a more durable surface when necessary.

Dolomite, pieces of clean limestone, is bright white, and in squares combined with other materials this surfacing is dramatic. But with wear, dolomite discolors and must be replaced.

Crushed brick has a bright-red color that gives a striking accent to planting. The brick eventually breaks down and wears away. Yet it is perhaps the best of the loose-fill materials for durability.

Gravel or marble chips conform to the contour of the ground and are strictly temporary pavings. Loose gravel or pebbles or granite wash out of place, so use a high border to keep these materials confined— wooden strips or bricks are fine.

To install a loose-fill material, dig out 6 to 8 inches of ground. Cover the area with heavy polyethylene plastic to keep weeds out. Then pour 2 to 3 inches of fine gravel over the plastic. Put the chips in place, level, and rake them so that the surface is easy to walk on.

Plastic stones coated with vinyl are yet another recent innovation for outdoor coverings. In many colors, the stone is made from igneous rock and can be used for paths, driveways, and patios. The material is said to be fade-proof and will not chip or chalk for seven to twelve years. It is nonallergenic and nontoxic to plants and people, and it is available in 50- and 100-pound waterproof bags.

38

Installation is simple. A shallow bed is prepared, and the stones are laid in place and then raked or brushed level with a board. Edging strips can also be put down to keep the stones confined.

OTHER PAVING MATERIALS. Slate is available in rectangles, squares, or irregular pieces and in numerous colors, and it makes a striking floor. Slate has a slightly textured finish, is resistant to strain, and comes in 1-inch or ½-inch thicknesses. It is elegant in appearance and lasts a lifetime, but it is rarely inexpensive.

Fieldstone makes a casual floor because of its natural variations in shape, texture, and color. Select flat stones for the upper side, with bottom irregularities sunk into the ground. The success of the pattern depends upon your patience in fitting and aligning the stones properly.

Flagstone is hard, stratified stone (sandstone, shale, slate, or marble) split into flat pieces. It may be laid dry on a sand base or in mortar. For masonry installation use stone 1 inch thick; for dry laying, 1½ inches thick.

3. Patio Roofs and Overhangs

A patio that has a partial roof or overhang becomes an additional living area. The roof affords protection from weather and adds further dimension to the patio. Design the structure so that it is safe and can support sufficient weight as well as wind pressure. In areas where the snow is heavy you must also be sure the roof can support the snow load.

Most patio overheads are constructed with beams, rafters, and posts, with a covering such as wood, canvas, reed, louvers, and so forth. Once the basic frame is built you can choose a covering for it.

CONSTRUCTION

1. Lay out the lines of the patio roof on the patio floor. Be sure the corners are square.

2. Mark the post locations with stakes on the patio floor and prepare footings for the posts (dig down at least 18 inches or more, depending on local frost lines). Set the posts in concrete.

3. Establish the post locations; leave 16 inches between the posts for most construction.

4. Set the posts in place; use a line level and carpenter's level.

5. Mark on the house all the roof lines of the patio cover.

6. Attach the ledger to the house wall.

7. Match the posts to the height of the ledger.

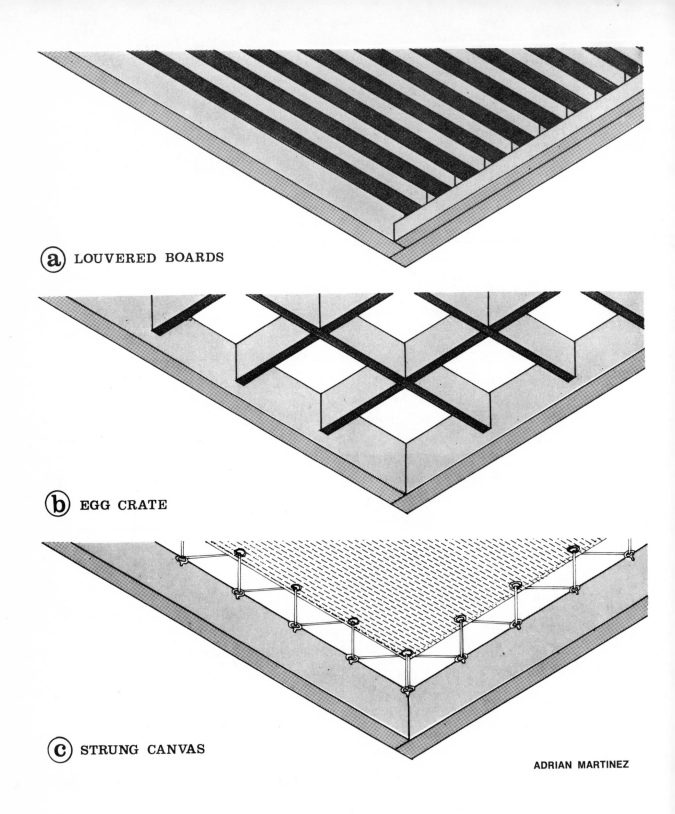

ⓐ LOUVERED BOARDS

ⓑ EGG CRATE

ⓒ STRUNG CANVAS

ADRIAN MARTINEZ

Patio Overheads

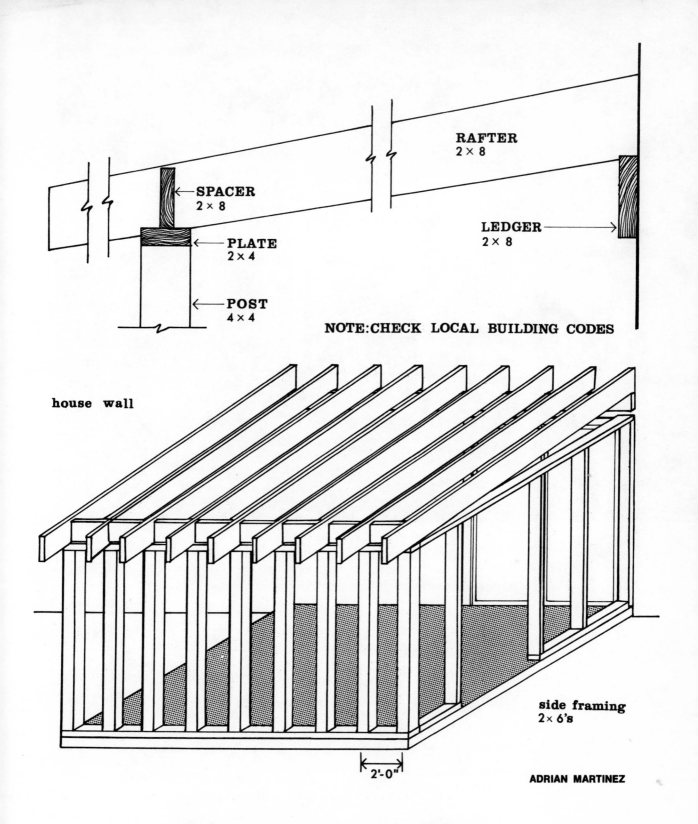

SPACER
2 × 8

RAFTER
2 × 8

PLATE
2 × 4

LEDGER
2 × 8

POST
4 × 4

NOTE:CHECK LOCAL BUILDING CODES

house wall

side framing
2× 6's

2'-0"

ADRIAN MARTINEZ

Enclosing a Patio

35. The overhead for this patio/porch is 4-by-4 Douglas fir posts, 4-by-6-inch beams, 2-by-6-inch joists to support a translucent roofing. The overhang has made this area completely charming. (*Photo courtesy Western Wood Products*)

HINTS ON MATERIALS

1. Try to design structures with lengths of rafters, beams, and posts in even inches because this is the way lumber is sold.

2. Use common-dimension lumber such as 2 by 4, 2 by 6, and so on or 4 by 4, 4 by 6, and so on. Other sizes may not be considered stock and will cost more.

3. Always design the overhead with some concept of what you will cover it with. Many materials such as fiber glass come in stock sizes; prime for these dimensions.

4. When purchasing lumber, specify the grade, quantity, type of wood, size, and length in that order.

RAFTERS, BEAMS, POSTS, BRACING

Rafters and beams carry the roof load to the posts, and rafter sizes are the easiest to determine. The width of the roof becomes the rafter length, then the center-to-center spacing of the beams is figured. Beams run lengthwise and a general rule for figuring beam size is: for a 4-foot span a 4-by-4-inch beam is needed; for a 6-foot span, use a 4-by-6-inch beam; for an 8-foot span, a 4-by-8-inch beam; and so on. These are general dimensions for temperate climates; in areas where snow load is heavy, rafters and beams will have to be heavier. Beams throw the weight load

36. A simple redwood strip ceiling creates great drama in this enclosed patio area. Of lath house design, it serves beautifully to house plants and is pleasant to view. (*Photo courtesy California Redwood Association*)

to the posts, which then carry it to the foundation or building piers.

The universal post is 4 x 4 inches. It supports a very heavy roof load and only in rare circumstances will you need a heavier post unless the patio is so large that a heavier post is more in proportion to the total structure.

For most patio overhangs or roofs, the wall of the house is used as a support and the point of connection is of vital importance. Generally the overhead shelter is attached to the main house with a sloping roof and eave line. The patio roof can be attached to the roof, a wall, or in some cases the eaves. You can determine the best way for your own personal situation. Be sure to build the roof high enough so it clears swinging doors and windows.

Attaching the overhead structure to the house wall is the easy method

37. This roof is 2-by-2-inch Douglas fir supported on 2-by-5-inch beams. The overhead enclosure makes a living area out of a barren space. (*Photo courtesy Western Wood Products*)

of construction and if your eave line is high enough you can set the rafters under the gutter and anchor directly into the house wall. The simplest way to do this is to fasten a long board to the house wall where rafters can rest. This "ledger" will carry the weight and should be anchored securely to the studs with lag screws or spikes. Fasten the ledger to the studs where there is wood to lock into. In any other area the ledger will give way. Studs are generally 16 or 18 inches apart. Or use a stud finder (available at hardware stores) to find the wood.

If the wall is textured or stuccoed you will have to drill holes to attach screws or lag bolts. Use a masonry bit in a power drill. If the wall is concrete or brick be sure to drill in at least 2 to 3 inches and then fit the lead sleeves into the holes. To anchor the rafters on the ledge you can rest them on the wood and toenail them in place, or better yet use metal joist holders, which give a more solid support (available at lumber yards).

If you attach the overhead structure to the eaves or facing strip be extremely careful. These areas are generally the weakest possible point for supporting additional weight. In this case use metal fastening strips to assure that the rafters stay in place. In some cases where the fascia is thin stock it is better to remove it; add a 2-inch stock board.

To anchor the overhead to the roof (and this is a good way because it allows free escape of warm air from a patio), follow this method. Lay the ledger strip on the shingles or composition roof and attach it with lag bolts run through the roofing to the roof rafters. Now toenail the roof rafters to the ledger. Attach the ledger strip above the wall of the house to distribute the extra weight evenly and not strain the roof. Be sure to caulk this line so leakage of water doesn't occur.

INSTALLING RAFTERS.   The rafters support their own weight and the weight of the covering material. Because most rafters will be a fairly long span they can twist or bend. Thus, crossbracing with blocks will be needed. Use a series of 2-by-6- or 2-by-8-inch blocks to hold 2 by 6s or 2 by 8s in place. Or use 2 by 4s placed against the top of each rafter.

Rather than place the posts on the outer rim of the patio overhang, it is aesthetically more pleasing to allow some overhang. The overhang should be in proportion to the structure and should be neither too long nor too short. Use the table on p. 46.

RAFTER SPACING CENTER TO CENTER	LUMBER DIMENSIONS			
	2 by 4	2 by 6	2 by 8	2 by 10
16	2 ft.	3 ft.	4 ft.	5 ft.
24	1 ft.-8 ins.	2 ft.-8 ins.	3 ft.-6 ins.	4 ft.-6 ins.
32	2 ft.-6 ins.	2 ft.-6 ins.	3 ft.-2 ins.	4 ft.

Most roofs will be pitched so rain can run off freely and the slope need not be more than ¼ inch per foot. To construct a pitched roof after the ledger strip is in place and the beams and posts are set, lay a rafter board so it rests on edge on both beam and ledger. Then force the tip snugly against the house wall and mark the end for cutting to conform to the wall. Now cut the triangular piece off the rafter end and rest the cut rafters so it is angled and fits snugly against the wall. Using the triangular piece of wood cut from the tip as a template, mark the rafter to be cut where it rests on the ledger strip and the beams. Using the first rafter as a template cut all other rafters accordingly. Then toenail the rafters into place. Use a sealer preservative between the surfaces of the joints before nailing.

INSTALLING BEAMS.   There are several ways of attaching the beam to the post but the simplest method is to rest it on top of the post and fasten it with straps or by toenailing. You can also see metal connectors or post caps or joist hangers or ledgers.

Although there may be a temptation to rest one or both ends of the beam against the house, support is necessary elsewhere. Give the beam support independent of the house wall. This is done by using posts (a separate one for each beam if possible) set out from the wall and resting on their own footing. Or if this isn't possible use a 4 by 4 alongside the house wall on its own footing.

SETTING POSTS.   The 4 by 4 is the standard post and works well in almost all situations, or use a pair of 2 by 4s with separating blocks. Set posts in concrete or on precast piers (available at lumber yards). To do

38. Here a roof was added over part of a deck to provide shade. Metal strap brackets hold beams off the roof and 2-by-8-inch wood joists extend to posts and beams out on the deck. The added ceiling structure makes an ordinary porch extraordinary. (*Photo courtesy Western Wood Products*)

your own foundation, figure a pier of 14 inches deep and 12 inches wide. If the post attaches to a concrete floor, drill a hole in the concrete for an expansion plug and lag bolt to hold a metal anchor. (Post anchors are available at lumber yards.)

Until rafters have been placed on posts, the posts may be wobbly, so brace them accordingly with wood bracing or wires until beams and rafters are in place.

BRACING. To be sure wind does not destroy the overhang or roof it is necessary to use bracing to make it structurally sound. A grid structure would normally have its own bracing by its design. If you don't have this type of roof use knee braces at the corners of posts, or steel rods in criss-cross fashion, or plywood if necessary.

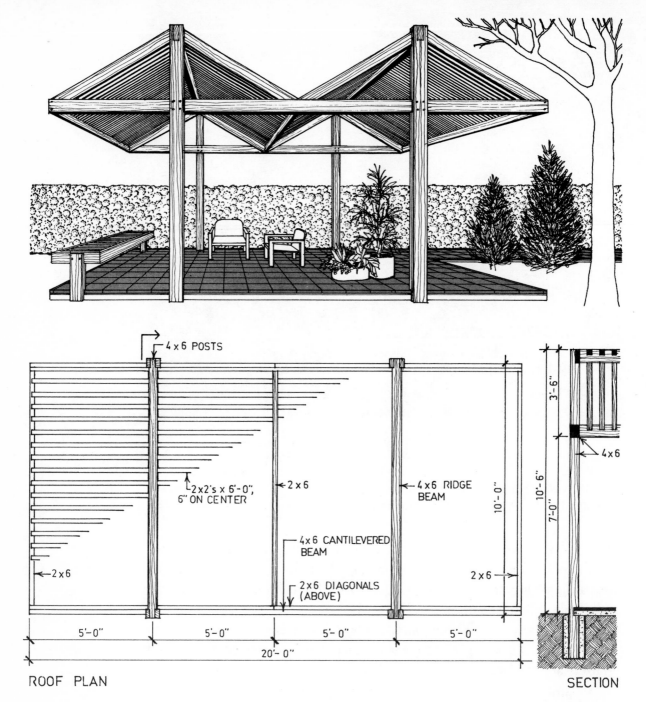

ROOF PLAN

- 4 x 6 POSTS
- 2x2's x 6'-0", 6" ON CENTER
- 2 x 6
- 4 x 6 RIDGE BEAM
- 4 x 6 CANTILEVERED BEAM
- 2 x 6 DIAGONALS (ABOVE)
- 2 x 6
- 2 x 6

5'-0"   5'-0"   5'-0"   5'-0"

20'-0"

SECTION

3'-6"   4 x 6   10'-6"   7'-0"   10'-0"

NOTE: THE TRELLIS ROOF IS DOUBLE PITCHED; 4x6 POSTS SUPPORT 4x6 RIDGE BEAMS AND CANTILEVERING SIDE BEAMS WHICH ARE CONNECTED BY 2x6 DIAGONALS. THE 2x2x6' LATH SPANS BETWEEN THE RIDGE BEAMS AT THE TOP AND 2x6's AT THE BOTTOM. POSTS ARE SET IN CONCRETE FOUNDATIONS. ALL LUMBER IS REDWOOD.

Redwood Trellis Overhead

design/drawing: Adrián Martínez

WOOD OVERHANGS

Here are some of the inexpensive kinds of wood to use over framing previously discussed:

Lath. This is outdoor rough-surfaced redwood or cedar ⅜ to 1⅝ inches in width and sold in lengths of 6 or 8 feet in bundles of 50. Ask for standard lathing lumber.

Batten. Battens are larger than laths milled to ¾ inches in widths of 2 to 3 inches. They can be bought in lengths of up to 20 feet and by the piece rather than the bundle. There are rough-surfaced battens and smooth battens.

Boards. Depending on your design you can use 1 by 4, 2 by 2, 1 by 2, or 1 by 3 boards in thicknesses of 1¼ inches. Construction-grade lumber is satisfactory, or if you want a more finished look kiln-dried lumber (20 percent higher in cost) can be used.

Trellis. Use 2-by-2-inch redwood carried on 4-by-6-inch beams; space them 6 inches apart. The double-eaved design is dramatic in the garden; use 4-by-6-inch posts.

Grapestake. Primarily a fence material, but these 2 by 2 rough-split pickets can be used for sturdy overhead too. Grapestakes are sold in 6-foot lengths.

LATH OR BOARD CONSTRUCTION. Any of the previously listed materials will have to run parallel to the wall to which the shelter is attached. To establish which direction the wood should run, decide what time of day you want maximum shade from the louver effect that laths cast. Run the lath east to west if you want noonday protection; if you need protection in the morning or late afternoon run the wood north-south. To space boards or laths for maximum efficiency follow these rules: Place lath ½ inch in thickness or less ⅜ to ¾ inch apart. For ½-to-1¼-inch lath, space it ¾ to 1 inch apart. If you use 2 by 2s the spacing can be 1½ to 2 inches apart.

Lath or board patterns can be checkerboard, grid, alternating widths, slanted, zigzagged, and so forth. There are many variations but don't overdo it. Simplicity is best. To determine how much lathing you need, figure the square footage of the area by multiplying width by length. Tell this figure to your lumber dealer and he will give you the correct amount of material.

Installing lath or board is quite simple and there are many choices. You can nail lath in place permanently or build a framework on the ground and then nail it in place. To space lath or board properly, after you have made the frame and nailed the first lath or board in place, lay down a board exactly as wide as the space you want, push the next wooden member against the guide board, and nail down both ends of the lath. Use as many nails as your patience will allow.

WOODEN LOUVERS. These deserve a section of their own because they are so suitable as a patio shelter. They block direct sunlight yet allow light through at other times of the day. The pattern they make is aesthetically pleasing, effective, simple; and if you decide to have adjustable louvers (a slightly more difficult installation), you have an almost perfect overhead.

A louver ceiling is made of parallel boards with boards set on edge or at an angle. If you place louvers running east and west you block midday sunlight and admit morning and afternoon sunlight, generally a good setup. If you set them in a north-south direction you admit morning or afternoon sunlight, depending on the angle of the louvers.

When you have decided on the angle of the boards you can build the cover of removable panels or attach the louvers directly to the framework overhead. In any case, the easiest way to proceed is to make a template (a small piece of wood) to act as a spacer. Nail the first louver in place, using the triangular guide, and then nail the rest of the louvers. You can also cut the rafters in steps and then put the louvers in place.

EGG-CRATE DESIGN. Next to the louvered-board overhead, the egg-crate design is the most handsome and satisfactory because it allows maximum sunlight and still affords a sheltered look. For eastern or northern exposure the egg-crate ceiling is ideal, it allows in most available sunlight, only cutting out early-morning or late-afternoon sun. While the egg-crate design will not temper the heat, it can be made to be more efficient by covering with plastic or cloth or by placing the boards so the egg-crate design is closely meshed.

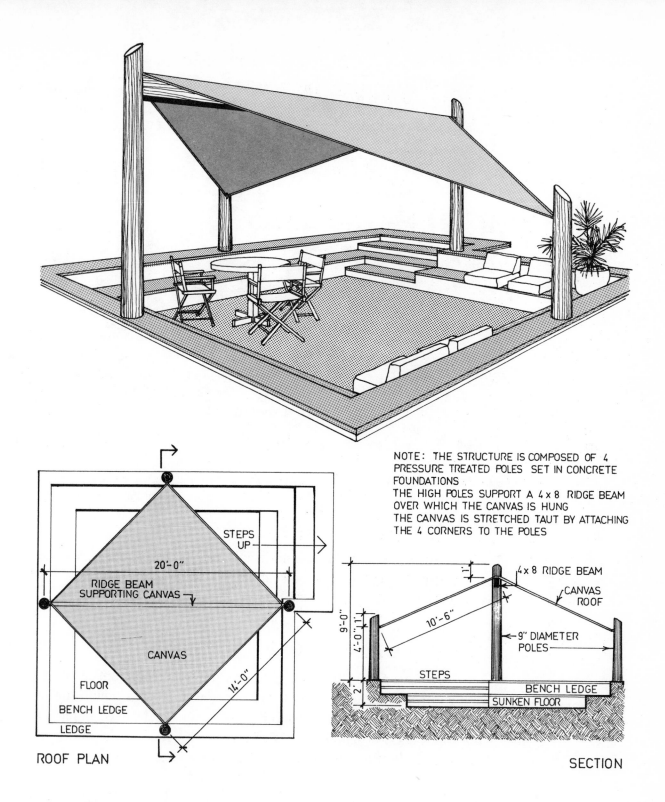

NOTE: THE STRUCTURE IS COMPOSED OF 4
PRESSURE TREATED POLES SET IN CONCRETE
FOUNDATIONS
THE HIGH POLES SUPPORT A 4 x 8 RIDGE BEAM
OVER WHICH THE CANVAS IS HUNG
THE CANVAS IS STRETCHED TAUT BY ATTACHING
THE 4 CORNERS TO THE POLES

STEPS
UP

20'-0"

RIDGE BEAM
SUPPORTING CANVAS

CANVAS

14'-0"

FLOOR

BENCH LEDGE

LEDGE

ROOF PLAN

4 x 8 RIDGE BEAM

1'

CANVAS
ROOF

9'-0"

10'-6"

4'-0"

9" DIAMETER
POLES

2'

STEPS

BENCH LEDGE

SUNKEN FLOOR

SECTION

Canvas Overhead

design/drawing: Adrián Martínez

39. A very handsome overhead was achieved by running canvas on metal poles. Note the handsome design of the screening. (*Photo courtesy American Canvas Institute*)

The egg-crate ceiling is easy to install and you can simply mark the spacing you want on the two end rafters. Then stretch a chalk line between the marks. Repeat for each row for blocking.

CANVAS AND AWNINGS

If you have always thought of canvas for only store-front awnings, give it another thought as an overhead material. Canvas is now made in many new designs, colors, and fabrics and is an excellent covering for patio overheads. Furthermore, it is easy to work with, can be drawn or closed with little effort, and in the newer designs is especially handsome.

There are many different weights, finishes, and weaves in canvas cloth and new processes of making it so it does not deteriorate in sun and rain. It lasts many years. For overhead use a 10.10-ounce weight generally called duck cloth, which comes in rolls of standard dimensions.

Although there are several types of colored canvas, painted canvas or plain off-white is very desirable. Vat-dyed canvas should be avoided because it does fade in sun.

No matter how good the canvas, just how it is used will determine its life expectancy, but in general a good-quality vinyl canvas will last between five and seven years.

Be selective about material for overheads. As mentioned there are many, including cotton sheeting, burlap, denim, vinyl-coated, and so forth. It pays to shop to get the best. Cotton, burlap, and denim, for example, will not last as long as canvas (although they are cheaper).

THE FRAMEWORK.   Generally canvas is strung on a pipe skeleton for installation. Pipe framework is easy to put together and is available from hardware stores or canvas suppliers. Standard galvanized water pipe is used for posts, rods, and rafters and is generally ¾ inch in diameter. Pipe can be threaded at your hardware store and is relatively inexpensive, and all in all this can be a reasonable cost item for a patio overhead. The

40. Using awnings in frames, a unique overhead was created for this deck. The triangular design is handsome and interesting. (*Photo courtesy American Canvas Institute*)

41. Canvas is stretched above this entryway to provide color and protection from rain and sun. The total effect is very pleasing. (*Photo courtesy American Canvas Institute*)

special fittings you will need to join the parts of the framework together are at the awning supplier. You will need:

1. A rod and rafter holder for attaching to the house

2. Slip tees for joining three pieces of pipe

3. Post plates or flanges for supporting the base of the post

4. Ells for right-angle corners

Most awning shops will be happy to figure out how much hardware you need if you tell them the square footage of the area you are covering.

42. Striped awnings provide a nice decorative note to this garden landscape. (*Photo courtesy American Canvas Institute*)

43. An unusual draped canvas repeats the espalier pattern of plants on wall and acts to make this a cohesive scene. (*Photo courtesy American Canvas Institute*)

Use smaller lengths of canvas such as 5 by 5 feet rather than a large sheet of 10 by 10 feet, which is more readily thwarted by wind. The pipe installation is quite simple:

1. Set up the ledger against the house wall (as you would for other overheads).

2. Fasten rod-and-rafter holders against the ledger at points where pipe will be, generally at ends and then on 17-inch centers.

3. Use ¾-inch pipe to span the width of the area (do not go over 15 feet long).

4. Secure a parallel pipe to the house-wall ledger and fasten with ells at ends and screw tees in centers.

5. Set the posts in post plates; use 1-inch pipe for the posts.

ATTACHING CANVAS. There are several ways of attaching the canvas to the pipe. It can be sewed with nylon thread or laced; the most efficient way is to have grommets in the canvas and the nylon thread strung through the grommets. The awning shop will furnish canvas with grommets. The trim look of lacing on canvas is especially handsome and this has many advantages. Installation is simple and you do not have to wrestle with many pieces of pipe and bales of canvas as when you sew it on. The lace method is simply stringing cord through the grommets and back to the pipe in a continuous zigzag or lace-on pattern. It is almost as easy as a lacestitch in sewing.

PLASTIC PANELS

Plastic panels of rigid fiber glass have become popular for patio overhangs and they do have pluses. They are inexpensive, come in many colors, and installed properly are not objectionable to the eye. They also admit light, depending upon the colors you select, or can be an opaque color to block out light.

Plastic is also lightweight and easy to install. Panel sizes range from 24 to 60 inches in width and 8 to 20 feet in length—a large selection.

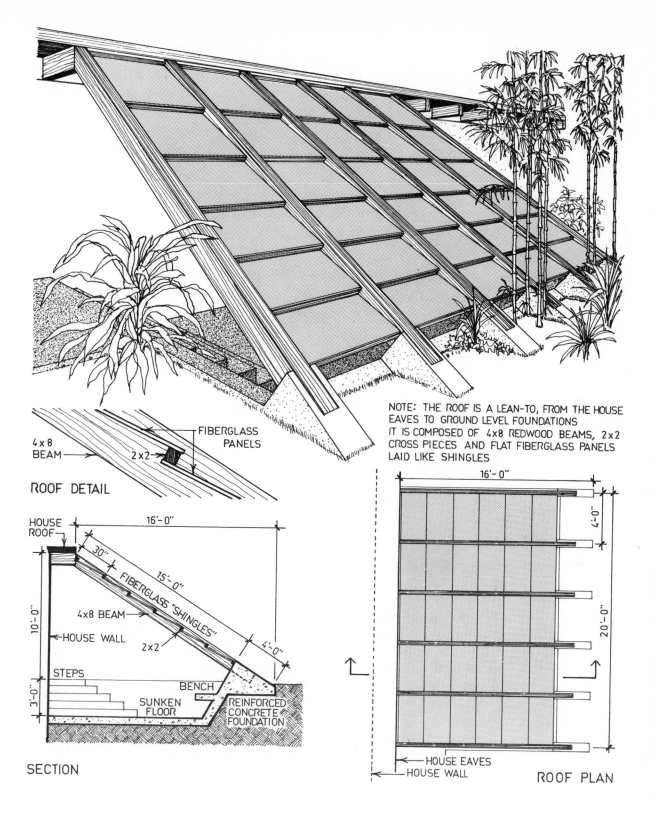

ROOF DETAIL

4 x 8 BEAM

2 x 2

FIBERGLASS PANELS

NOTE: THE ROOF IS A LEAN-TO, FROM THE HOUSE EAVES TO GROUND LEVEL FOUNDATIONS IT IS COMPOSED OF 4x8 REDWOOD BEAMS, 2x2 CROSS PIECES AND FLAT FIBERGLASS PANELS LAID LIKE SHINGLES

HOUSE ROOF

16'-0"

30"

15'-0"

FIBERGLASS "SHINGLES"

4x8 BEAM

10'-0"

HOUSE WALL

2x2

4'-0"

STEPS

3'-0"

BENCH

SUNKEN FLOOR

REINFORCED CONCRETE FOUNDATION

SECTION

16'-0"

4'-0"

20'-0"

HOUSE EAVES

HOUSE WALL

ROOF PLAN

Fiberglass Overhead

design/drawing: Adrián Martínez

INSTALLATION. The popular corrugated or flat panel is 26 inches wide and if you space rafters 2 feet on center (usually done), this allows a 2-inch overlap, which is fine. Support the panels along the seams and use weatherproofing compounds to seal the joints before you nail them in place.

Crossbracing will be needed every five feet between the rafters to support the panels across the corrugations. The egg-crate frame 2 feet wide and 5 feet long with the corrugations running lengthwise works well.

Plastic panels can easily be sawed and drilled; use the special aluminum twist nails for installation. Drive nails through the crowns, not the corrugations, on 12-inch centers.

A variation of a fiber glass fence, and a handsome one, is to use flat fiber glass panels laid like shingles. Cut the panels with a saw. This is a dramatic design, and we show how to build it in the drawing, p. 57.

OTHER OVERHEAD MATERIALS

Aluminum screening. This screening has a long life expectancy under normal usage, is lightweight, and is moderately priced. It needs no varnish or paint and is easily installed.

Plastic screening. This is a plastic material with mesh insert. It does not corrode and is unaffected by humidity or salt air. Life expectancy is several years. Comes in standard widths of 24, 36, or 48 inches by the roll.

Aluminum and plastic screening. This is plastic-coated aluminum wire. The horizontal wires are broad and thus reduce temperatures. The material is easy to see through from the inside, yet affords daytime privacy.

Glass-fiber screening. A woven product with yarn coated with vinyl in a range of colors. It is stronger than metal and lightweight. Comes in widths to 64 inches in rolls.

Galvanized screening. The strongest of all metal screening but will rust in time. Still, because of its strength it has its uses.

4. Fences

Fences are more important to the garden than most people realize. Indeed, they can make a garden attractive or make it uncommonly ugly. There are dozens of fence designs. Select a good design and put your best workmanship into it, because it pays off in looks and durability. And another consideration: fences are not just barriers to block off an area, they are an integral decorative feature of a garden, large or small, and may be in any pattern and of any shape on the property.

However, before you start to plan your fence remember that local building codes dictate fence construction as to height and placement in relation to setbacks from streets. Also of prime importance are your neighbors and their property, or fences built between adjoining landowners. Many times a survey is necessary to determine where a fence can be located.

Only after you have decided on the kind of fence and have checked building codes is it time to actually lay out the fence. And this is best done on paper so you can rectify any errors easily before construction.

LOCAL BUILDING LAWS

Local building codes vary greatly from state to state. In some locales there are restrictions on using a high fence to enclose a front yard. The legal reasons vary but essentially make good sense, so do check first with local authorities. Some areas may have a restriction on wire fences of a hazardous nature—barbed-wire and electrical fences, in particular—and the use of glass fences is also restricted in many states. In addition, in some places the planning office may require that you erect a fence. This

59

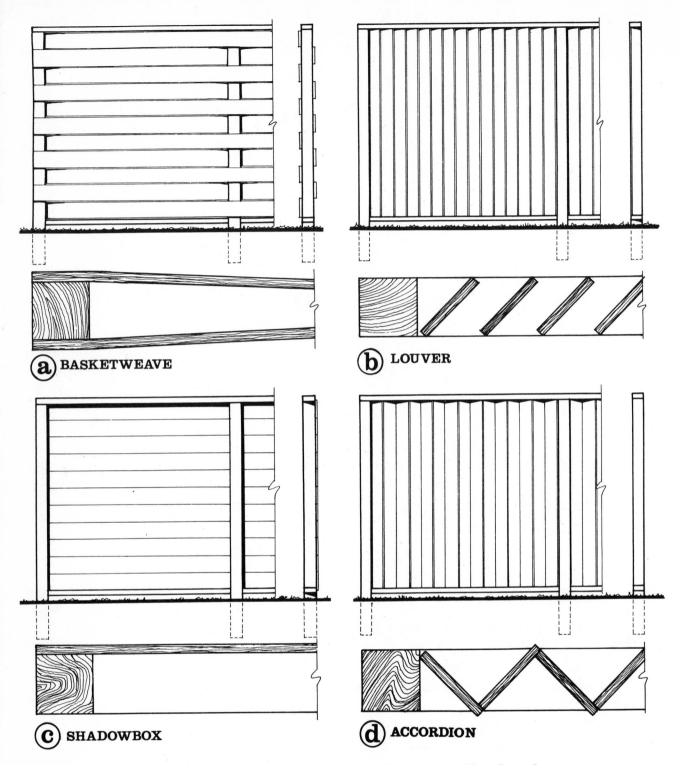

(a) BASKETWEAVE

(b) LOUVER

(c) SHADOWBOX

(d) ACCORDION

note: posts - 4x4's rails - 2x4's boards - 1x6's all redwood

ADRIAN MARTINEZ

Types of Fences

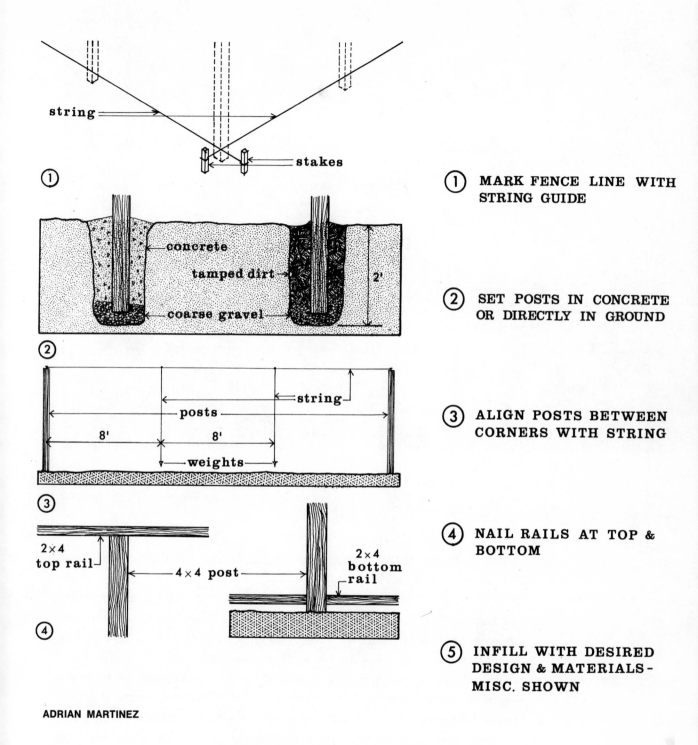

string

stakes

① MARK FENCE LINE WITH STRING GUIDE

concrete

tamped dirt

2'

coarse gravel

② SET POSTS IN CONCRETE OR DIRECTLY IN GROUND

string

posts

8'   8'

weights

③ ALIGN POSTS BETWEEN CORNERS WITH STRING

2×4 top rail

4×4 post

2×4 bottom rail

④ NAIL RAILS AT TOP & BOTTOM

⑤ INFILL WITH DESIRED DESIGN & MATERIALS - MISC. SHOWN

ADRIAN MARTINEZ

Building Fences

44. A louvered fence is attractive and has the advantage of allowing air to pass through it while still providing privacy. (*Photo courtesy Western Wood Products Association*)

is especially true for swimming pools in California; these areas must have fences to prevent accidents.

It is a good idea to consult with the neighbors of adjoining property (if there are any) about the fence and design. They may share the cost of a common-land fence or have a helpful idea or two. (Also, telling neighbors there is going to be a fence can avoid problems with them later.) Walk the property and lay out the corner stakes first by hammering them into the ground at specified points. Then run nylon string or twine between the stakes and tie it securely to the stakes. With these lines set you can now drive in stakes for the post holes. Place the post holes every 6 to 8 feet, depending upon the fence design you choose.

Once all stakes are in and the fence is more or less mapped on the ground, dig the post holes. For this you will need a digging tool like an auger or clam-shelled post-hole digger. No matter which tool you choose, digging into soil is hard work. In fact, if your fence is a long one, or if the soil is badly caked, investigate the possibility of renting a power digger. This is not an easy tool to handle, but if you have average strength, after some practice you will get the hang of it. If the surface is very rocky you will have to rent a jackhammer.

For most fences you will have to dig post holes at least 24 inches to 30 inches deep. The deeper the post is set in place the stronger your fence will be. A good general rule is to sink posts into the ground at least one-third their length. Make the bottom of the post hole wider than the top so there is a good solid base for the post (the width of the post hole should be twice the diameter of the post), and insert 2 to 4 inches of gravel at the bottom of the hole. The gravel will eliminate any water that accumulates at the bottom (which can cause wood to rot).

To set the post in place (this is called plumbing the post), shovel some gravel into the hole and put the post on top of it. Add several shovelfuls of concrete, juggle the post slightly, and then check the two

45. This partial vertical wood fence helps delineate the small grass patio area. Without the fence addition the area would hardly be pleasing. (*Photo courtesy Western Wood Products*)

sides with the level. If the post is not correct, move it slightly and correct the alignment. Use a lean concrete mix: 1 part cement, 3 parts sand, and 6 parts gravel (see chapter 6). The mix should be rather dry, never runny. Once it is aligned, hold the post by hand for a few minutes. It takes about 15 minutes for concrete to harden; do not nail on stringers (horizontal timbers) for at least 36 hours.

BUILDING THE FENCE

The actual building of the fence varies with the design used and who builds it. I put all posts in place, attach stringers, and then nail the vertical members in place. For a simple fence this is a good procedure.

Another method is to assemble the fence in sections—fitting in the

46. In some cases where bold definition is wanted a horizontal board fence is the answer; it supplies needed mass and creates dimension. Here a work storage center is included as part of the fence. (*Photo courtesy Western Wood Products*)

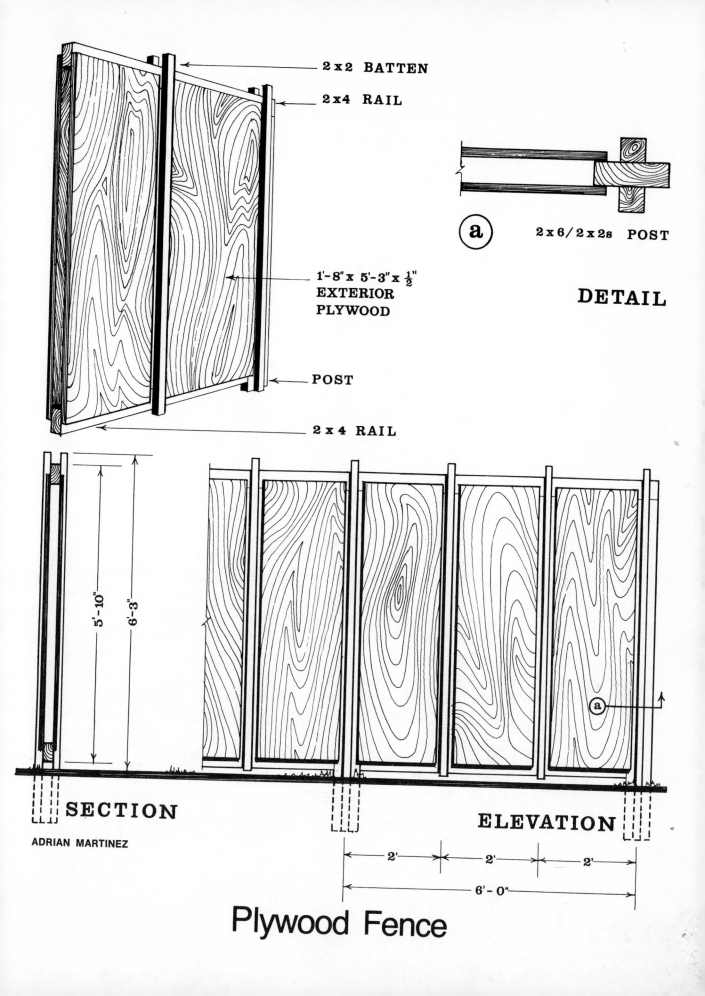

2 x 2 BATTEN

2 x 4 RAIL

a

2 x 6 / 2 x 2s POST

DETAIL

1'-8" x 5'-3" x ½"
EXTERIOR
PLYWOOD

POST

2 x 4 RAIL

5'-10"

6'-3"

a

SECTION

ADRIAN MARTINEZ

ELEVATION

2'

2'

2'

6'-0"

Plywood Fence

HIRING A FENCE COMPANY

Having someone do the job for you after you have supplied the design of the fence you want saves much time and labor. But it is not cheap. The prices I have gotten from most fence contractors were extremely high, but remember that if you go this route, the fence goes up quickly, and you do not lift a finger. If you hire professional help, have a written contract made specifying the grade of lumber to be used, the types of preservatives for the wood posts, how deep the posts are to be sunk, whether the posts are to be in concrete or soil, and so forth. Everything should be spelled out so there is no problem later when the work is in progress. Written agreements are worth their weight in gold; verbal agreements are often forgotten.

WOOD FENCES

Basically the fence made of wood is the most popular one. Whether you choose a lattice, board-and-batten, ranch, or picket fence (becoming very popular now), it should complement the garden.

KINDS. Fences can be classed as rail, split, post-and-rail, post-and-board, lapped-joint, slat, louver, board (plywood or redwood), basket-weave, and lattice. This sounds like many, and it is. Let us look at some of these designs and see what they can or cannot do for your garden.

A rail or timber fence is heavy in appearance and fine for large landscapes; it is easy to build and inexpensive but rustic in looks. The diagonal board fence is handsome; here the boards are used almost like sculptural components and this is a fence that requires some know-how—it is for the person handy with tools. The plywood fence with insets of redwood vertical strips is excellent when you are spanning a long area; the open space breaks the monotony of a very long fence.

The picket fence is fine as a low barrier, say 3 or 4 feet tall, but it does not provide complete privacy or very much protection from the wind. It is more decorative than functional, but for the colonial house or variations of it, a picket fence makes a handsome addition. Pickets are built with standard-sized boards such as 1 by 2, 1 by 3, or 1 by 4 inches.

The rail fence is fine for the country scene, where privacy is no factor and the horizontal design fits well into rolling or flat terrain. It is generally economical and easy to build, but it is not decorative or good for privacy.

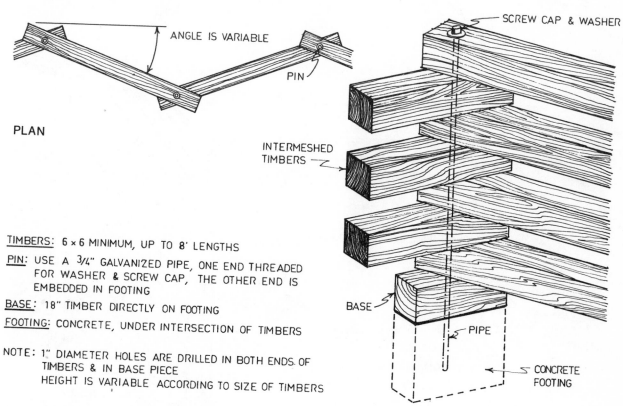

PLAN

ANGLE IS VARIABLE

PIN

SCREW CAP & WASHER

INTERMESHED TIMBERS

BASE

PIPE

CONCRETE FOOTING

<u>TIMBERS</u>: 6 × 6 MINIMUM, UP TO 8' LENGTHS

<u>PIN</u>: USE A 3/4" GALVANIZED PIPE, ONE END THREADED FOR WASHER & SCREW CAP, THE OTHER END IS EMBEDDED IN FOOTING

<u>BASE</u>: 18" TIMBER DIRECTLY ON FOOTING

<u>FOOTING</u>: CONCRETE, UNDER INTERSECTION OF TIMBERS

NOTE: 1" DIAMETER HOLES ARE DRILLED IN BOTH ENDS OF TIMBERS & IN BASE PIECE
HEIGHT IS VARIABLE ACCORDING TO SIZE OF TIMBERS

Timber Fence

drawing: Adrian Martinez

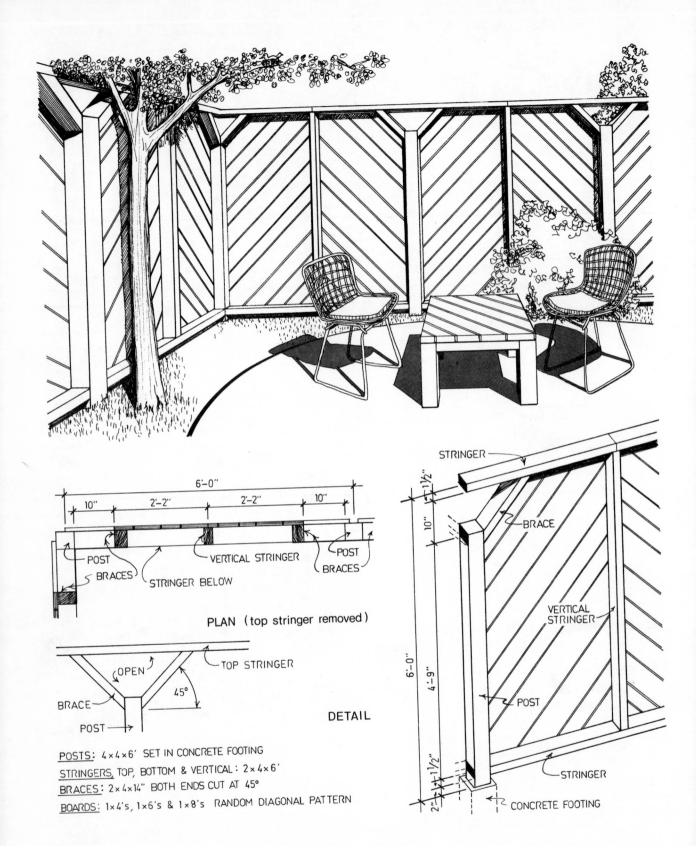

PLAN (top stringer removed)

DETAIL

POST
BRACES

VERTICAL STRINGER

POST
BRACES

STRINGER BELOW

6'-0"

10"   2'-2"   2'-2"   10"

OPEN

BRACE

POST

TOP STRINGER

45°

STRINGER

BRACE

VERTICAL STRINGER

POST

STRINGER

CONCRETE FOOTING

6'-0"

4'-9"

10"

1½"

1½"

2"

POSTS: 4×4×6' SET IN CONCRETE FOOTING

STRINGERS, TOP, BOTTOM & VERTICAL: 2×4×6'

BRACES: 2×4×14" BOTH ENDS CUT AT 45°

BOARDS: 1×4's, 1×6's & 1×8's RANDOM DIAGONAL PATTERN

Diagonal Board Fence

design/drawing: Adrian Martinez

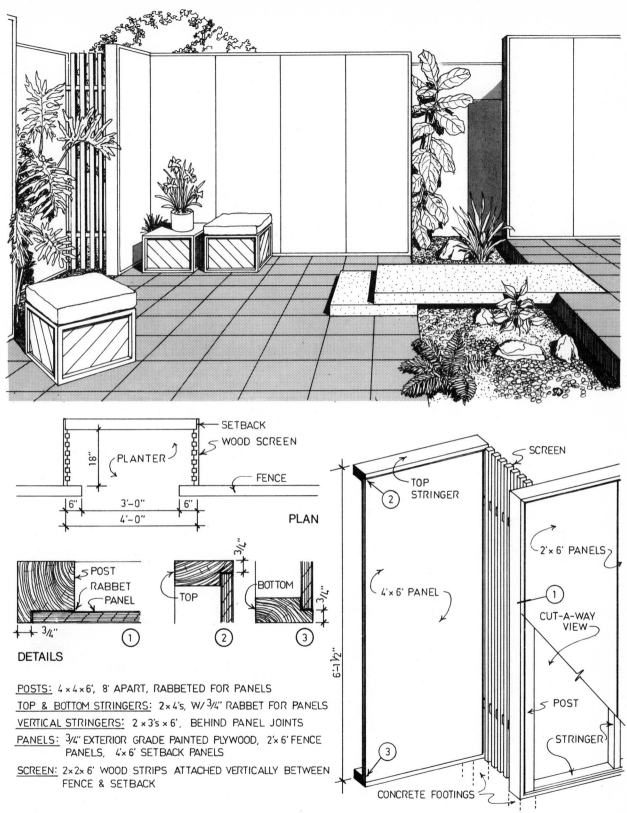

PLAN

SETBACK
WOOD SCREEN
18"
PLANTER
FENCE
6"   3'-0"   6"
4'-0"

DETAILS

POST
RABBET
PANEL
3/4"
①

3/4"
TOP
②

3/4"
BOTTOM
3/4"
③

SCREEN
TOP STRINGER
②
2'× 6' PANELS
4'× 6' PANEL
①
CUT-A-WAY VIEW
6'-1½"
POST
③
STRINGER
CONCRETE FOOTINGS

POSTS: 4 × 4 × 6', 8' APART, RABBETED FOR PANELS
TOP & BOTTOM STRINGERS: 2 × 4's, W/ 3/4" RABBET FOR PANELS
VERTICAL STRINGERS: 2 × 3's × 6', BEHIND PANEL JOINTS
PANELS: 3/4" EXTERIOR GRADE PAINTED PLYWOOD, 2'× 6' FENCE PANELS, 4'× 6' SETBACK PANELS
SCREEN: 2 × 2 × 6' WOOD STRIPS ATTACHED VERTICALLY BETWEEN FENCE & SETBACK

Plywood Fence

design/drawing: Adrian Martinez

This is a real pioneer-period fence, when wood was plentiful and boundary lines were flexible. These fences require only casual workmanship and may be in a zigzag design or split-rail. Post-and-rail design is sometimes seen too. But basically, the rail fence is not a good solution to today's properties.

Slat fences are simple to build, contribute greatly to a site, and look handsome in almost any situation. Material generally used is rough-finished redwood sawed into 1-by-1-inch or 1-by-2-inch strips. The design is somewhat formal but always neat, and these fences can provide complete privacy. Tests indicate that an open-slat fence provides very effective wind control, with closely spaced slats breaking up and dispersing the wind. Slats can be run vertically close together or spaced apart. They can also be used horizontally for a different look or even in combination with vertical slats for a dramatic effect. In the simplest application slats are nailed over a post-and-stringer frame. All in all, a slat fence is a good usable barrier, easy to build, and always pleasing.

If you need a windbreak and still want a good-looking fence, consider the louver design. By fixing the louvers accordingly you can still have maximum light, and shade too. And when faced across the path of prevailing winds a louver fence will temper the wind but still allow air circulation.

Vertical-spaced louvers give some privacy but part of the garden will always be visible through the fence as a person moves along it. For complete privacy, use the horizontal design. The louver fence has a strong architectural look and should be carefully matched to the design of the house itself. Buildings with simple, square, clean lines seem to be in keeping with the louver design.

With louver fences you will need a larger amount of material than with any other wooden fence. Also, because the louvers are supported only at the ends, warping and twisting might occur. Thus, many times expensive kiln-dried lumber is used. This is a heavy fence too, and the structure requires substantial posts and foundations. Yet even with its problems a louver fence is a handsome addition to the property.

The designs and variations of board fences are limitless, and this is a simple fence to build. The solid design provides maximum privacy but often creates a boxed-in look, so use it only for small areas. A better idea is to space boards, say ½ to 1 inch apart; or if privacy is a prime factor, instead of setting boards together leave space and then cover the vertical spaces with 1-by-1-inch boards to create a design. Boards placed slantwise within

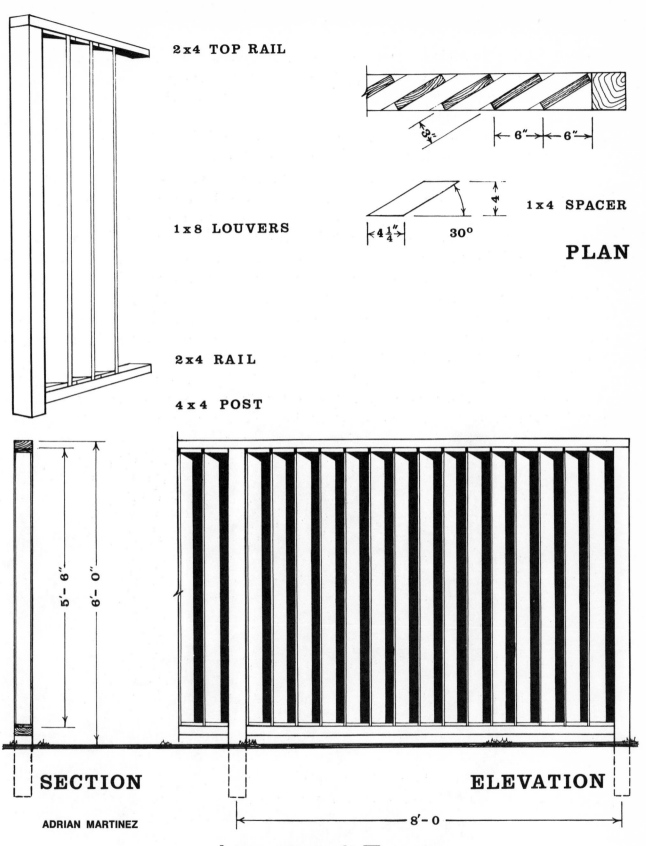

2x4 TOP RAIL

1x8 LOUVERS

2x4 RAIL

4x4 POST

6"

6"

3"

4

1x4 SPACER

4 1/4"

30°

PLAN

5'- 6"

8'- 0"

SECTION

ELEVATION

8'- 0

ADRIAN MARTINEZ

Louvered Fence

the frame also provide an interesting variation. Thin batten designs, either horizontally or vertically, in somewhat of a trellis effect, can provide eye interest and result in a handsome design. The board fence can fit into almost any landscape plan (the exact design will depend on the house itself and the boundary lines).

Board fences are generally easy to build; a sturdy post-and-rail frame is made and the boards are attached in easy fashion. Use 6-by-6-inch or 4-by-4-inch posts set 6 to 8 feet apart; 2 by 4s can serve as rails. These fences are heavy, so be sure to use substantial foundations for them.

The attractive appearance that the basketweave fence gives on both sides makes it quite popular. The design may be horizontal or vertical, and the weave can vary from flat to very wide and open. Triangular de-

49. An inexpensive vertical board fence was used in this difficult landscape situation. At levels, the total fence design works well. It provides needed privacy and delineation for the garden. (*Photo courtesy Western Wood Products*)

50. There is no reason why fences have to be vertical or horizontal; in a diagonal pattern, this redwood fence is quite handsome. (*Photo courtesy California Redwood Association*)

signs using thin wooden strips can also be done. Rough-finished lumber is usually preferred and strips should not be thinner than ½ inch or thicker than 1 inch. A favorite width is 6 inches and length can vary from 14 to 18 feet.

When viewing the basketweave fence it looks complicated to build but actually it is not. Many times rails are not used and it is simply a matter of nailing strips at posts. Cost is minimum and dealers offer prefabricated panels of basketweave fencing and all you need do is nail it to posts.

Trellis or lattice fences really have more use than at first glance. Depending upon the lumber—heavy or light—and the grids—close together or far apart—this type of fence provides many versatile designs and always looks handsome. A tightly woven lattice fence can give complete privacy. A slightly open design allows air to circulate. All in all, the trellis fence is quite adaptable and imparts an elegant, almost Victorian feeling to a property. However, these fences are not easy to construct and require painstaking attention to detail.

51. Shadow-box areas are incorporated in this handsome fence and the results are most pleasing. The open areas provide places for plants. (*Photo courtesy California Redwood Association*)

Panel fences made of hardwood pressed board or more popularly of plywood offer several advantages: the fence goes up quickly, there is a wide range of materials to use, and panels give complete privacy. You will need strong structural support for this fence and it is wise not to use it in very long expanses, for it will be confining.

Plywood is the best material for a panel fence and comes in several thicknesses and sizes; the 4-by-8-foot size is the best. (Always specify exterior grade.)

PLANTER FENCES

Generally we think of fences as straight lines in one dimension, to be planted later, perhaps with vines. However, the place for plants (planters) can be incorporated into the design of the fence for a very effective picture.

Openings in the frame, somewhat like frames on a wall, can also be built into a fence and thus provide a place for hanging plants. Framed openings may be narrow or wide, depending upon the size of plant you intend to use. Aesthetically, three openings in a row are more attractive than, say, a single opening by itself. Step fences are still another way of creating a distinctive fencing and also incorporating planters.

OTHER FENCE DESIGNS

Pole fences patterned after Japanese-designed structures are another possibility and afford a distinctive note to a garden. They are more open than most fences but have a simple elegance that is suitable for many properties. Here the posts are round rather than square and this lends a different look that is appealing.

52. To create a finished look, coping and moldings were added to this wood fence and the structure becomes architectural in character; this is sometimes required depending on the character of the home. (*Photo courtesy California Redwood Association*)

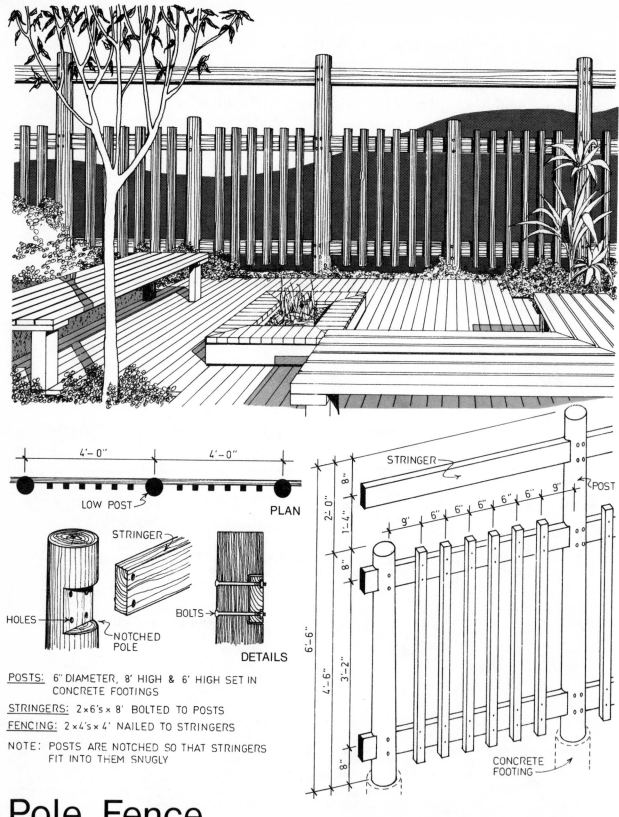

PLAN

4'-0"   4'-0"

LOW POST

STRINGER

HOLES

NOTCHED POLE

BOLTS

DETAILS

POSTS: 6" DIAMETER, 8' HIGH & 6' HIGH SET IN CONCRETE FOOTINGS

STRINGERS: 2×6's × 8' BOLTED TO POSTS

FENCING: 2×4's × 4' NAILED TO STRINGERS

NOTE: POSTS ARE NOTCHED SO THAT STRINGERS FIT INTO THEM SNUGLY

STRINGER

POST

8"   2'-0"   1'-4"   8"   3'-2"   4'-6"   6'-6"   8"

9" 6" 6" 6" 6" 9"

9" 6" 6" 6" 6" 9"

CONCRETE FOOTING

Pole Fence

drawing: Adrian Martinez

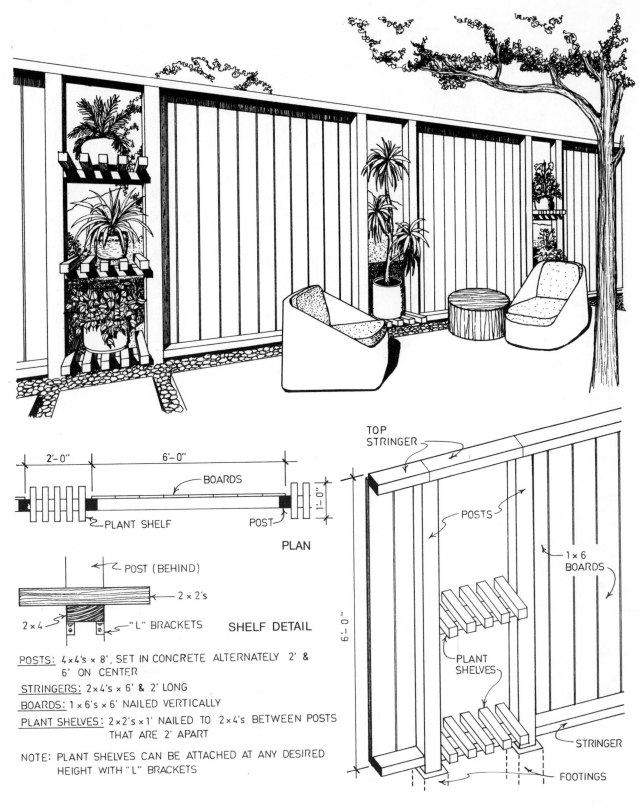

2'-0"   6'-0"

BOARDS

1'-0"

PLANT SHELF   POST

PLAN

POST (BEHIND)

2 × 2's

2 × 4   "L" BRACKETS   SHELF DETAIL

POSTS: 4×4's × 8', SET IN CONCRETE ALTERNATELY 2' & 6' ON CENTER

STRINGERS: 2×4's × 6' & 2' LONG

BOARDS: 1×6's × 6' NAILED VERTICALLY

PLANT SHELVES: 2×2's × 1' NAILED TO 2×4's BETWEEN POSTS THAT ARE 2' APART

NOTE: PLANT SHELVES CAN BE ATTACHED AT ANY DESIRED HEIGHT WITH "L" BRACKETS

TOP STRINGER

POSTS

6'-0"

1 × 6 BOARDS

PLANT SHELVES

STRINGER

FOOTINGS

Plant Shelf Fence

design/drawing : Adrian Martinez

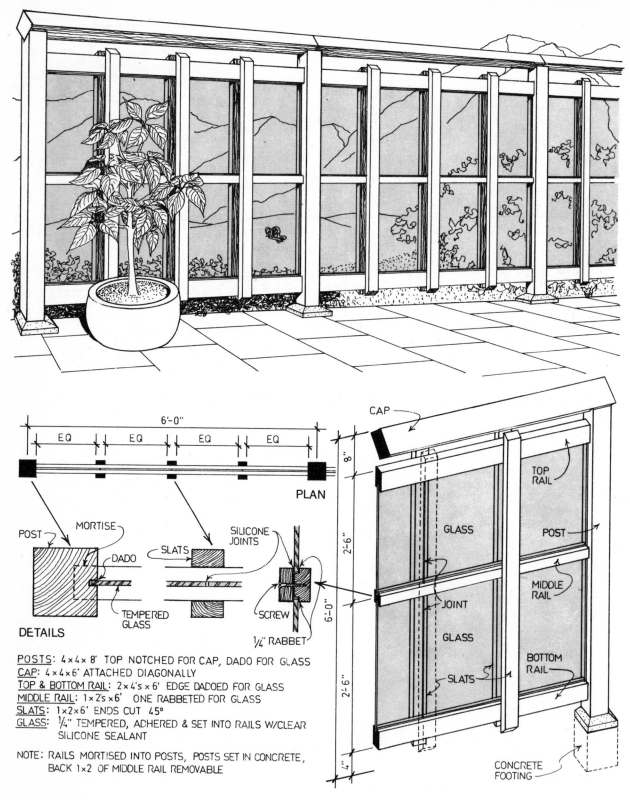

6'-0"

EQ | EQ | EQ | EQ

PLAN

DETAILS

POST

MORTISE

DADO

SLATS

SILICONE JOINTS

TEMPERED GLASS

SCREW

¼" RABBET

CAP

8"

2'-6"

6'-0"

2'-6"

4"

TOP RAIL

GLASS

POST

MIDDLE RAIL

JOINT

GLASS

BOTTOM RAIL

SLATS

CONCRETE FOOTING

<u>POSTS</u>: 4 × 4 × 8' TOP NOTCHED FOR CAP, DADO FOR GLASS
<u>CAP</u>: 4 × 4 × 6' ATTACHED DIAGONALLY
<u>TOP & BOTTOM RAIL</u>: 2 × 4's × 6' EDGE DADOED FOR GLASS
<u>MIDDLE RAIL</u>: 1 × 2's × 6' ONE RABBETED FOR GLASS
<u>SLATS</u>: 1 × 2 × 6' ENDS CUT 45°
<u>GLASS</u>: ¼" TEMPERED, ADHERED & SET INTO RAILS W/CLEAR
    SILICONE SEALANT

NOTE: RAILS MORTISED INTO POSTS, POSTS SET IN CONCRETE,
    BACK 1 × 2 OF MIDDLE RAIL REMOVABLE

Glass & Wood Fence

design/drawing : Adrian Martinez

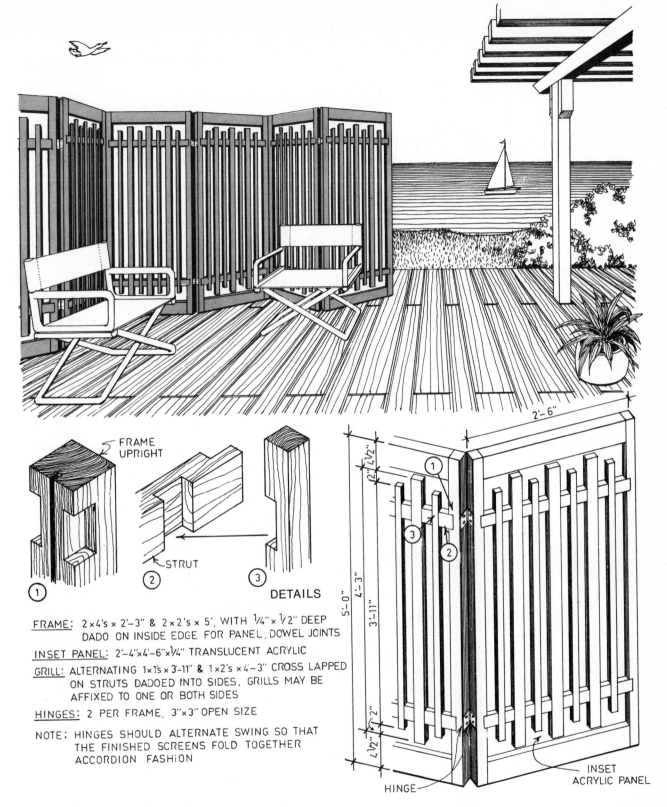

FRAME UPRIGHT

STRUT

① ② ③

DETAILS

FRAME: 2×4's × 2'–3" & 2×2's × 5', WITH ¼" × ½" DEEP
    DADO ON INSIDE EDGE FOR PANEL, DOWEL JOINTS

INSET PANEL: 2'–4"×4'–6"×¼" TRANSLUCENT ACRYLIC

GRILL: ALTERNATING 1×1's × 3'–11" & 1×2's ×4'–3" CROSS LAPPED
    ON STRUTS DADOED INTO SIDES, GRILLS MAY BE
    AFFIXED TO ONE OR BOTH SIDES

HINGES: 2 PER FRAME, 3"×3" OPEN SIZE

NOTE: HINGES SHOULD ALTERNATE SWING SO THAT
    THE FINISHED SCREENS FOLD TOGETHER
    ACCORDION FASHION

2'–6"

2" 4½"

5'–0"

4'–3"

3'–11"

2"

4½"

① ② ③

HINGE

INSET
ACRYLIC PANEL

Moveable Fence

design/drawing: Adrian Martinez

A plant-shelf fence is both a fence and a place for plants and the unique design offers the gardener numerous possibilities for plant arrangement. The green islands of the fence create a totally lovely look and these fences are as easy to build as a standard fence. The plant shelves are redwood slats placed at 6-foot intervals. The distance from shelf to shelf (horizontally) can of course be varied depending on the length of the fence. Long fences need more plant shelves than, say, a standard 20-foot expanse.

Perhaps the most difficult fence to make is a wood-and-glass one, but where you want to have a view this kind of fence is the answer. The fence is basically tempered glass glazed in wood sash. It is a heavy fence and must be built with adequate supports (see drawing p. 82). You can substitute ¼-inch acrylic sheets for the glass to avoid the weight factor.

Still another fence idea is a movable screen, and this is indeed a convenience because it can be removed at will to another location if it is not suitable in a specific place. It will take you longer to make a movable-screen-type fence but it does have benefits in the garden—for example, to block wind, to afford privacy where and when you want it.

53. Here, canvas is used as a fencing material in combination with wood, and the results are handsome. (*Photo courtesy National Cotton Council*)

5. Walls

The terms "walls" and "fences" may seem synonymous, but they are not, because a wall can do many things a fence cannot. For example, walls can be used within a garden to define an area, such as a low wall at the edge of a flower border. But walls can also define property in the same way a fence does. Yet by their very nature—stone, brick, cement—walls impart still another character to a site. A 6-foot brick wall substantially deadens sound or acts as protection against hot sun. In addition, walls—especially brick and stone—have an old-time quality that is charming in a garden.

You can tackle small decorative walls for breaking the property (up to 3 feet) by yourself. This means digging and pouring concrete that is not beyond the average person. But high solid-concrete walls will require foundations and should be built by professionals. Making wood forms and pouring great amounts of concrete can be tricky for the novice.

Check local building codes about walls, heights, and frost lines (how deep you have to dig to install a solid foundation so freezing will not crack the wall), and also check to see if a building permit is necessary.

KINDS

There are as many designs for walls as there are for wooden fences. Brick is the most popular material, but concrete and decorative blocks, cement, and stone are other good materials. Design will of course vary with the material, and each wall will give the property a different look. The brick wall is perennially charming and well suited to large property but too heavy for small sites. The concrete-block wall (of the right design) fits almost any situation, as do decorative blocks. Stone walls are infinitely

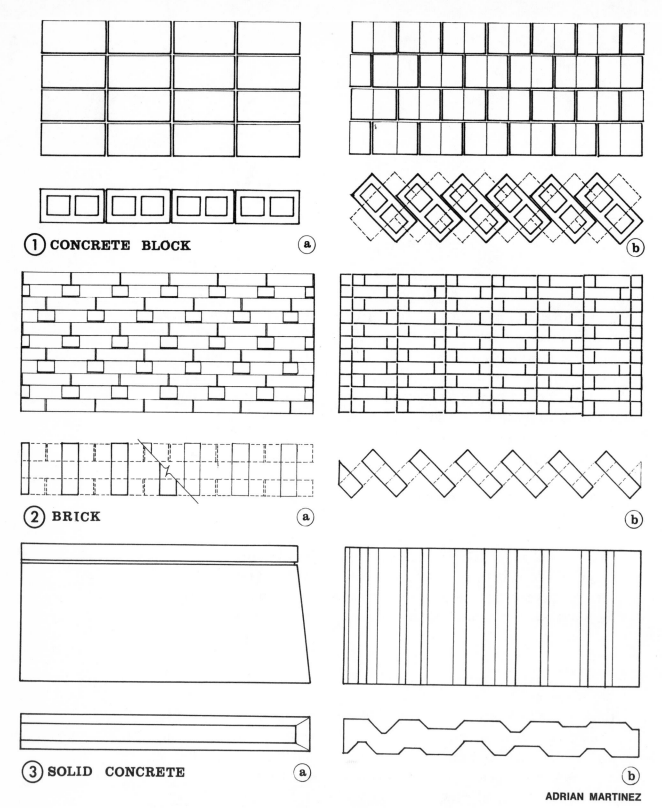

① CONCRETE BLOCK   ⓐ   ⓑ

② BRICK   ⓐ   ⓑ

③ SOLID CONCRETE   ⓐ   ⓑ

ADRIAN MARTINEZ

Patio & Garden Walls

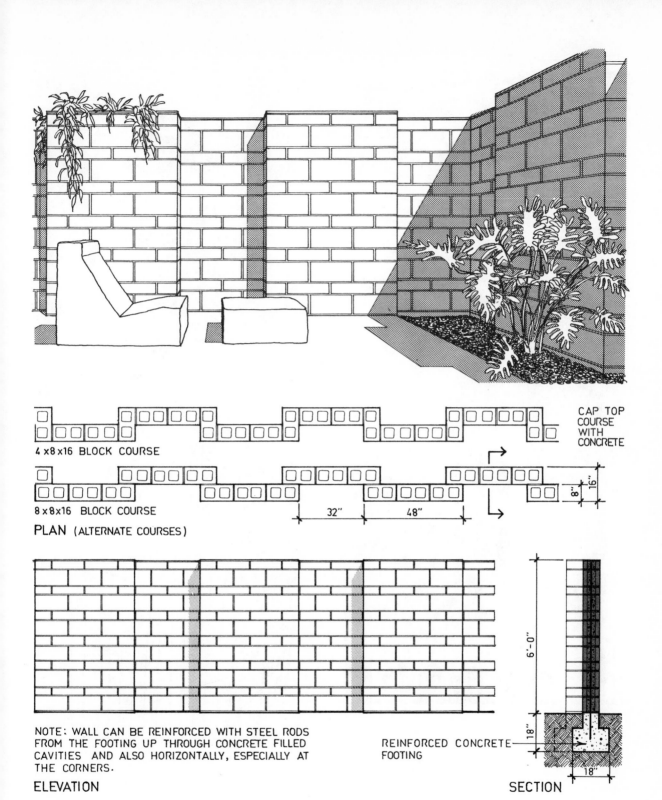

4 x 8 x 16 BLOCK COURSE

8 x 8 x 16 BLOCK COURSE

PLAN (ALTERNATE COURSES)

CAP TOP
COURSE
WITH
CONCRETE

32"　48"

8"　15"

6'-0"

18"

18"

REINFORCED CONCRETE
FOOTING

SECTION

NOTE: WALL CAN BE REINFORCED WITH STEEL RODS
FROM THE FOOTING UP THROUGH CONCRETE FILLED
CAVITIES AND ALSO HORIZONTALLY, ESPECIALLY AT
THE CORNERS.

ELEVATION

Concrete Block Wall

design/drawing: **Adrián Martínez**

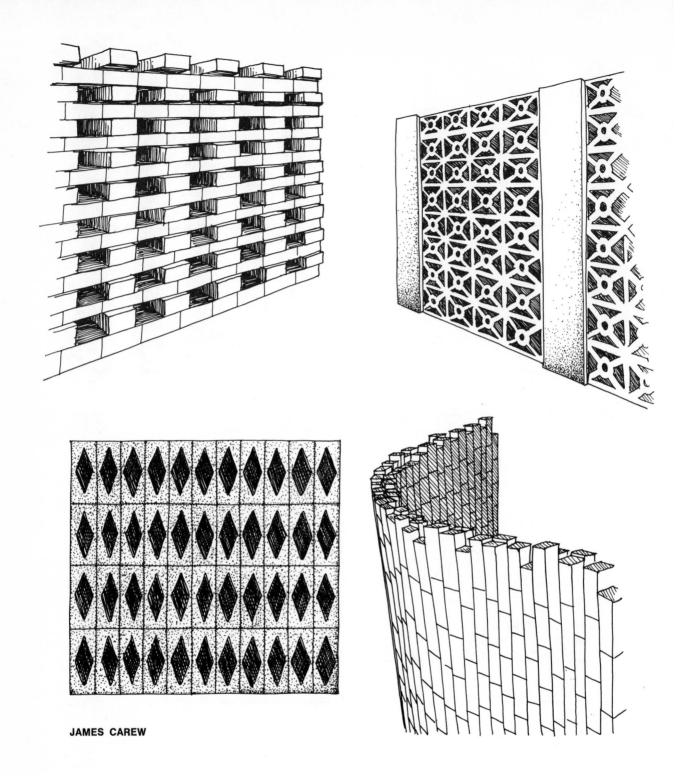

JAMES CAREW

Designs of Decorative Blocks

handsome and provide a rustic look; they are fine for most properties (but not all).

The easiest walls to build are those of concrete or decorative blocks. This is a comparatively rapid procedure, and the average handy person can do it.

CONCRETE AND DECORATIVE BLOCK

For walls, block is the most exciting and versatile of building materials. There are blocks with color (green or tan) cast in them, or you can paint them with rubber-based masonry paints or use them in their natural gray color by waterproofing them with a silicone liquid. There are patterned and textured blocks that can be used in a great variety of designs—stacked, staggered, running-bond, on-end. There are ordinary aggregate heavy blocks, but for walls you will want to use the lightweight kind because they give better insulation, more effectively deaden sound, and are easy to lift. The most common size is 16 inches long, 8 inches high, and 8 inches wide. Foot-square and 4-inch blocks are on the market, and blocks are also available in brick shapes, solid rather than hollow. In addition to the standard block there are half, corner, double-corner, bullnose, and channel blocks to help you make wall building easy.

If you are looking for a textured wall, select the textured split block and slump block. The split form has a rough face, and slump block has sags or slumps, lending itself to interesting dimensional effects. It is also possible to use two types of blocks in one wall to create an interesting pattern—for example, alternate a row of 8-inch blocks with 4-inch ones.

There are different ways of treating the mortared joints. A tooled joint is a sort of half-round cove or squeezed joint, where mortar is allowed to show between the joints. A raked joint produces a sharp relief; this is done by cleaning the mortar from the joint to a depth of ½ inch or less.

Decorative block (grille) is different and also very popular because each unit is a frame surrounding a grille, fretwork, or contoured design. Depending upon the pattern, the decorative screen-block wall may be very open or very closed. This has advantages because the design is invariably pleasing in comparison with a solid wall, and it provides air circulation and a modicum of privacy. The blocks are lightweight; inexpensive; easy to clean by hosing; impervious to fire, termites, or rust; and can be laid by the average person with little difficulty. Patterns range from Mediterranean motifs to Moorish designs. Most are indeed handsome and add considerable charm to the property.

INSTALLING A BLOCK WALL. A block wall needs a substantial footing (foundation) of concrete. The foundation may be 18 or 24 inches (check local frost lines). Pour the foundation in forms; when it is set, you can start the installation of block. Use just enough water to make the cement mix plastic so that it clings to the trowel and block without running or squeezing down when you lay the block. As you work you will learn the right consistency for the mortar. Lay out the blocks on the foundation without mortar, and shift them around until they fit. The idea is to save you having to cut blocks. Keep the spaces between the blocks no wider than ½ inch, no narrower than ¼ inch. Clean the foundation and wet it down. Now mix mortar, or use a plastic cement or a premixed mortar (you add only water). Now trowel on a 2-inch bed of mortar, and seat the first block. Tap it into place with the trowel handle. Repeat the process, putting mortar on the inside end of each succeeding block.

For a sturdier wall, lay the block on a footing that is still in a plastic state (consistency of mortar). The first course of blocks is then solidly attached to the foundation. When the concrete foundation has become like the consistency of mortar, it is ready for blocks. But first, as in any foundation, position the blocks on the ground alongside the foundation so you have enough blocks and little cutting is necessary. Then seat the block about 2 inches deep into the mortar. You want the foundation concrete still to be pliable so you can level the blocks. Start at the corner with a level and square-shaped corner block, and trowel mortar in strips on the outside edges of the first course. Do one block at a time, tapping each one into position. Always be sure it is level and flush with the block beneath. Keep the courses even with a mason line. (See the brick section, following, for mortar properties.) Put down just enough mortar for one block at a time.

If you place a wall where there is a drainage problem, you will have to put drain tiles along the outer edge. Slope the wall about 1 inch for each 15 feet. Be sure to cover the joints with roofing paper and backfill with gravel.

For tall walls (over 5 feet), use reinforcing rods set vertically and solidly in the concrete foundation. Space them according to local building

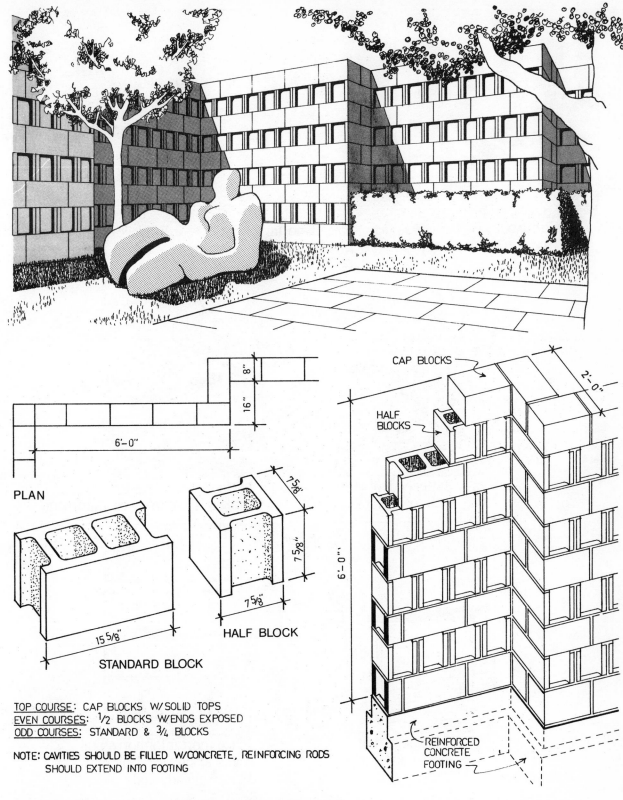

PLAN

8"

16"

6'-0"

7 5/8"

7 5/8"

7 5/8"

15 5/8"

STANDARD BLOCK

HALF BLOCK

CAP BLOCKS

HALF BLOCKS

2'-0"

6'-0"

REINFORCED CONCRETE FOOTING

TOP COURSE: CAP BLOCKS W/SOLID TOPS
EVEN COURSES: 1/2 BLOCKS W/ENDS EXPOSED
ODD COURSES: STANDARD & 3/4 BLOCKS

NOTE: CAVITIES SHOULD BE FILLED W/CONCRETE, REINFORCING RODS
SHOULD EXTEND INTO FOOTING

Concrete Block Wall

design/drawing : Adrian Martinez

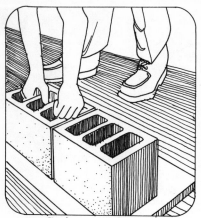
1. String out the block on the footing

2. Spread mortar for the first few blocks

3. Place the end block solidly in the mortar

4. Butter ends of face shells of each block

5. Use a mason's level or straight board to check alignment

6. Make sure that blocks are true

7. Place mortar for horizontal joints along face shells of blocks already laid

Concrete Block Wall Construction

codes. Lay the first course of the wall in wet concrete, and then drive the rods through the cores. The holes for rods must match the holes in the blocks, so alignment is vital.

A screen-block wall (one with designs) is laid on a foundation, and then the block is installed with epoxy mortars. These mortars are extremely strong, and thus generally no reinforcing rods are necessary. The tops and sides of the blocks are covered with epoxy (from a caulking gun) and blocks are set in place. All materials can be found at local building-supply houses.

BRICK

The beauty of brick cannot be denied; it is a natural material that harmonizes with most outdoor situations. Whether in a straight, L-shaped, or serpentine wall, brick offers charm and stands the test of time. Furthermore, brick offers a multitude of patterns: thin, thick, colored, rectangular.

The average brick wall is 8 or more inches thick (two bricks wide) and requires steel reinforcing rods in mortar joints at frequent intervals. Very large walls will have to be reinforced about every 12 feet with a brick pier or pilaster. This type of construction requires the help of a professional mason. You can dictate the pattern to suit your tastes, but the actual building of the wall (unless you are very handy with tools) generally must be farmed out. However, for those who want to try constructing their own brick wall, you will need these tools: pointed trowel for buttering mortar, broad-bladed cold chisel, hammer, level, and carpenter's square.

INSTALLING A BRICK WALL. Common brick must be damp to be laid. To hold the mortar you need a mortar board: a piece of wood, say a top of an orange crate. Scoop the mortar (enough for only a few bricks) from the board with the trowel, and spread it over the top course of bricks. Put each brick in place, trim away mortar to butter the end of the next brick, and continue until more mortar is needed. Bricks should be set in perfect alignment; tap them into place gently. Build the ends or corners first in steps because this will make it easier to set the next bricks in line. Be sure to use a strong guide line—that is, a nylon line to guide you in laying the bricks. Anchor the ends of the line into mortar joints. Before the mortar sets, trim away loose bits and smooth off all joints.

Mortar for bricklaying is a mixture of cement, fine sand, and water,

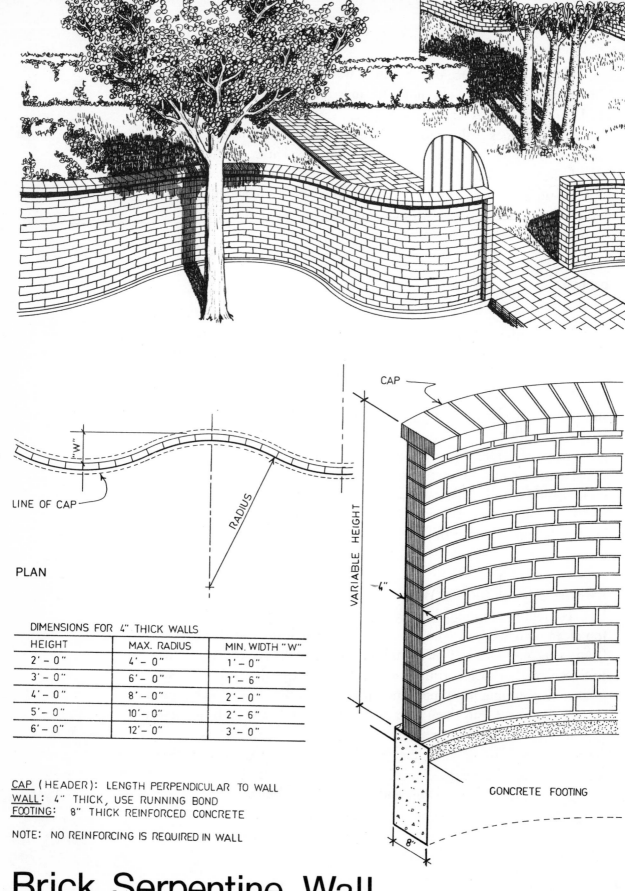

LINE OF CAP

PLAN

CAP

VARIABLE HEIGHT

4"

RADIUS

W

CONCRETE FOOTING

8"

DIMENSIONS FOR 4" THICK WALLS

HEIGHT	MAX. RADIUS	MIN. WIDTH "W"
2' – 0"	4' – 0"	1' – 0"
3' – 0"	6' – 0"	1' – 6"
4' – 0"	8' – 0"	2' – 0"
5' – 0"	10' – 0"	2' – 6"
6' – 0"	12' – 0"	3' – 0"

CAP (HEADER): LENGTH PERPENDICULAR TO WALL
WALL: 4" THICK, USE RUNNING BOND
FOOTING: 8" THICK REINFORCED CONCRETE

NOTE: NO REINFORCING IS REQUIRED IN WALL

Brick Serpentine Wall

drawing: Adrian Martinez

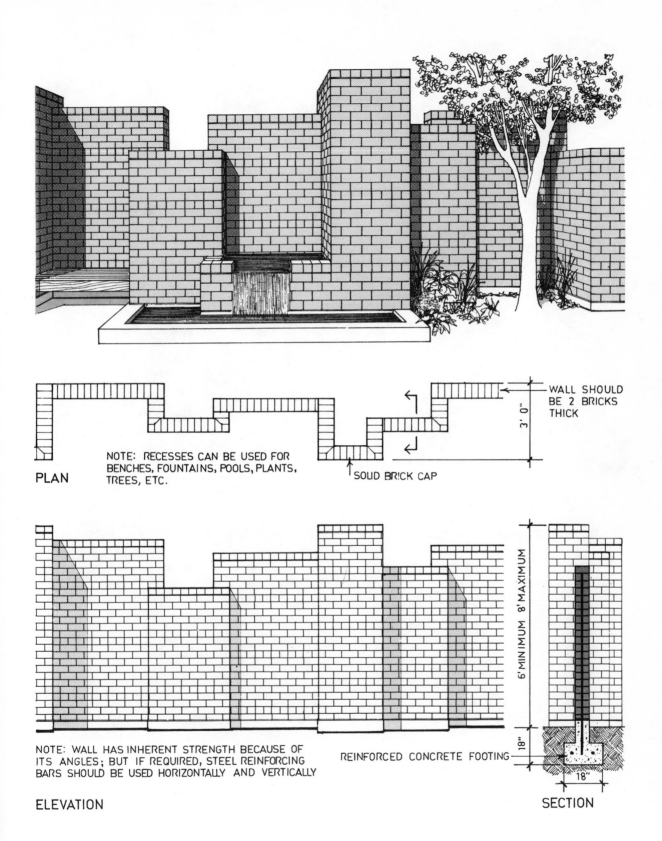

PLAN

NOTE: RECESSES CAN BE USED FOR
BENCHES, FOUNTAINS, POOLS, PLANTS,
TREES, ETC.

SOLID BRICK CAP

WALL SHOULD
BE 2 BRICKS
THICK

3' 0"

NOTE: WALL HAS INHERENT STRENGTH BECAUSE OF
ITS ANGLES; BUT IF REQUIRED, STEEL REINFORCING
BARS SHOULD BE USED HORIZONTALLY AND VERTICALLY

ELEVATION

REINFORCED CONCRETE FOOTING

6' MINIMUM 8' MAXIMUM

18"

18"

SECTION

Variable Brick Wall

design/drawing: Adrián Martínez

54. Brick walls have an old world character and blend well with wood houses; this step and wall arrangement really creates a pretty picture. (*Photo by Ken Molino*)

55. A rubble rock wall is used here to define the pool area and act as a retaining wall. The texture of the wall is pleasing. (*Photo by Roger Scharmer*)

with some lime added for plasticity: 2 parts Portland cement, 1 part fire-clay or lime, and 9 parts garden sand. Supplies are sold at hardware and lumber stores.

STONE

Building a stone wall is like putting a jigsaw puzzle together because each stone must be set into place perfectly. The skilled stoneworker can create a wall that appears as if each stone were precut before assembling. As an amateur you will have to be content with less than perfection because stone walls are difficult to build (but not impossible).

The beauty of stone walls is their natural look and their countrified character. And there are many beautiful stones to use: stratified rock such as limestone, shale, and sandstone are very pleasing, and granite and basalt rock are equally handsome.

INSTALLING A STONE WALL. Stone walls can be made of either uncut stones, known as rubble, or cut stones, known as ashlars. Unstratified stones are difficult to cut and thus are generally laid in rubble form. I

56. The rustic charm of rubble walls is pleasing and handsome in certain situations. Here the cobblestone paving acts as a perfect complement for the wall. (*Photo by Matthew Barr*)

think the rubble wall is more difficult to perfect than the ashlar type, because with rubble you have to fit and juggle, while ashlars are relatively simple to put in place.

When you are working with stone be sure of your design from the start; the wall should appear natural, as you would see the stones on the ground, never upended or in an awkward position. You will have to work as you go along with the design, so an eye for aesthetics is necessary. There is no set pattern for a stone wall; the design depends upon the stones used and your own personal judgment.

Like most walls, stone walls require a good foundation of concrete to avoid cracking and splitting. In cold climates the frost line is about 26 inches (check with local building codes). Start the actual stone structure a little below the surface of the ground, and lay it directly with mortar on the concrete foundation. If you decide to tackle your own stone wall (and let me warn you, it is not easy), here are some hints:

57. A simple masonry rock wall defines this property and the effect is handsome; the vertical masonry pillars supply a needed vertical accent. (*Photo by Matthew Barr*)

1. Keep plenty of stones ready. It is much easier to fit a stone in place when you have a choice rather than to force it in place.

2. Use plenty of mortar to fill in all joints. Where there are spaces fill in with chunks of stone and mortar over them.

3. String guide lines and keep the face of the structure flush.

CONCRETE

Concrete walls have many advantages: a poured wall can be almost any shape; it is extremely strong; and surface texture can be in several finishes, such as textured, smooth, or embossed. But cast concrete is hardly a job for the do-it-yourselfer. Precise forms are necessary, and careful pouring of concrete is essential to create a handsome wall. This particular kind of wall building is best left to professionals.

58. An architectural block wall has its merits, too, for the pattern is pleasing to the eye. This wall allows air to enter and still affords privacy for the homeowner. (*Photo courtesy National Concrete Masonry Association*)

RETAINING WALLS

Retaining walls do more than hold back a hill; they can and should be decorative too. A dry-stone-wall installation with plants in earth "pockets" is quite effective in the garden. So are cascading plants covering the sharp edges of masonry or wooden retaining walls.

An easy dry-wall method of installation is to place stones against a slope. Between the stones leave earth pockets. The stones should be chosen to pitch the wall back toward the thrust of the slope. Dry stone walls are not difficult to build and also offer the gardener the chance to grow small plants between the stones—a fascinating kind of gardening, very decorative for an area. Keep dry walls to a maximum of 4 feet. Higher walls are apt to tumble with time if there are severe rains.

A retaining wall of over 4 feet is not easily constructed and it is best to seek professional help with these structures. Remember that if the wall is not properly engineered and built, it might collapse after the first few rain storms. However, low walls, as mentioned, can be built by the average homeowner with little cost.

A main consideration of any retaining wall is that there is ample provision for water drainage. Soil absorbs a large quantity of water during a rainy season; it flows downhill below the surface. Where the water hits the wall it accumulates, building up pressure, and it may burst the wall.

Leaving weep holes in the wall is the simplest way of getting rid of excess water. Tile and gravel backfill will also prevent undermining of a wall. Where weep holes are used, construct a special gutter to carry off water so it doesn't ruin a patio or lawn. Standard drain tiles or rounded concrete gutters can be used. All gutters should be wide enough to shovel away debris—leaves, twigs—if necessary.

59. A very sophisticated patterned concrete block wall is used for drama and for privacy on this property. It adds mass and beauty to the landscape. (*Photo courtesy National Concrete Masonry Association*)

60. Textured block is frequently used for walls and can be used in many designs; this fretwork wall has visual appeal and makes a bold statement. (*Photo courtesy National Concrete Masonry Association*)

61. Elaborate block walls can also be used in some cases; installation of these modular blocks is easy and the total effect is dramatic. (*Photo courtesy National Concrete Masonry Association*)

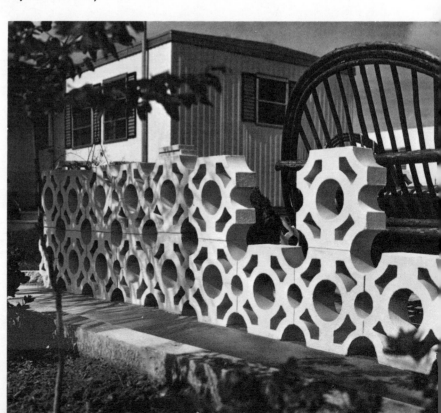

62. The fleur-de-lis pattern is handsome and comes in blocks for easy installation; a distinctive wall. (*Photo courtesy National Concrete Masonry Association*)

Again, let me say that where the wall is over 4 feet or the slope of the hillside more than 30 percent, seek outside help.

MASONRY RETAINING WALLS. A masonry retaining wall may be brick, concrete block, or cast concrete. In any event it is better to have a series of low walls than one high one—it is less likely to lean or break under pressure. Concrete foundations and reinforcing rods will be necessary with any masonry wall.

Brick retaining walls are lovely but they are difficult to build. Even when securely mortared they do not have the holding power of a concrete wall. Reinforcing rods are necessary in brick as are weep holes, and this is a job best left to the professional. However, for all their problems, a brick wall lends old world charm to a garden. So if it is your choice, have it built, but be sure it is built to stay.

WOODEN RETAINING WALLS. Redwood or cedar boards are frequently used for low retaining walls (terrace beds, too) and these are effective in appearance and function fine if built properly. However, even with these resistant woods, do use a fungicide preservative on any wooden member that comes into contact with the soil. Generally 2-by-12-inch boards are run horizontally and 4-by-4-inch posts support them. Dig deep post holes (about 28 inches) and use a gravel base as for regular fence work. Place posts every 4 feet for support; you might also want to brace the wall with wooden members.

Plant vines and trailers in the earth. In time they will drape the wall in rich green.

Generally, for wall footings and foundations you should use 6 gallons of water for each sack of cement. To mix the concrete add 2 shovelfuls of gravel and the same amount of sand to the concrete and mix. Add water from a garden hose, a little at a time, mixing as you go. Continue mixing all ingredients until they are well combined and of the desired stiffness. If you have added too much water, add some more sand, gravel, and cement. If the mixture is too thick, add more water. When using a hand or power mixer follow the same procedure.

63. A close-up of a grooved panel block wall which provides fine visual interest to property. (*Photo courtesy National Concrete Masonry Association*)

6. Decks

Decks are overlooked in garden construction and yet they are a worthwhile addition to any property and are especially useful on hillsides. Whether the deck is at a low level or on the side of a steep hill, it brings nature into the home. In any case, the deck must be built solidly and with careful consideration of weight factors. Decks ill constructed will be shaky and hardly desirable as an addition to the home. The general building codes on decks specify: "The floor must be designed to support 40 pounds per square foot of surface in addition to the weight of the deck."

Another consideration of decks is that they must have guard rails with a minimum height of 30 inches and be capable of resisting a load of 20 pounds per lineal foot acting at the top.

Building codes referring to decks will vary in each city and it is a good idea to check your local building office for specific information. The planning and construction offered here are general and not to be construed as any legal limitations.

Decks are usually of four kinds:

1. Platform in the yard

2. Hillside deck attached to the house

3. Rooftop decks

4. Ground-level decks (patios)

In each case the construction is somewhat different, and although concrete decks are often built, here we discuss wooden decks because the concrete deck is covered in the section on patios (page 14).

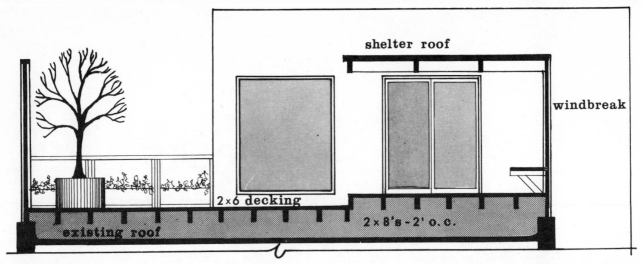

SECTION A

shelter roof

windbreak

2 × 6 decking

2 × 8's - 2' o.o.

existing roof

design: adrián martínez

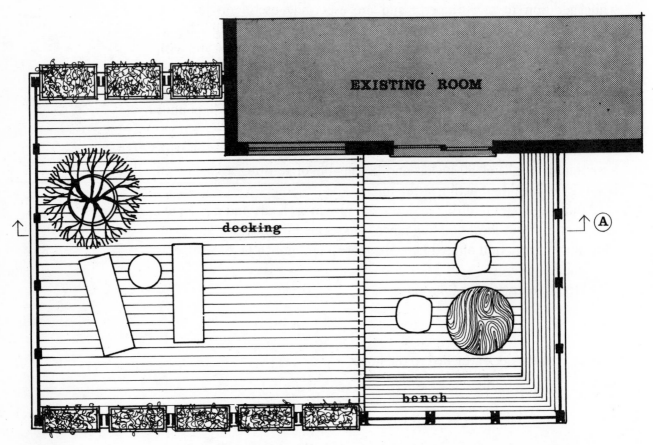

EXISTING ROOM

decking

bench

↑Ⓐ

PLAN

note: the new structure is supported on existing bearing walls

Roof Deck

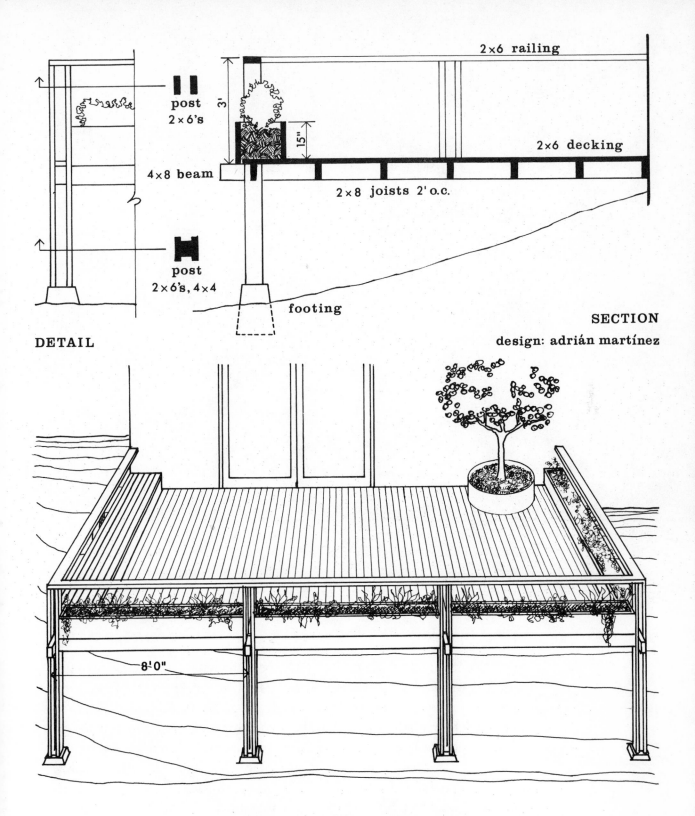

post
2×6's

3'

15"

post
2×6's, 4×4

4×8 beam

footing

2×6 railing

2×6 decking

2×8 joists 2' o.c.

DETAIL

SECTION
design: adrián martínez

8'0"

Hillside Deck

64. Two-by-four decking makes a handsome patio here. The wood decking blends well with the grass area and the elevated design provides dimension in the garden. (*Photo courtesy Western Wood Products*)

LOCATION

Scout the site to determine just where the best place for a deck may be; this will vary in each case. In the desert, for instance, cold northern light might be very desirable and a southern exposure a mistake. The best way to determine the location of the deck is to observe the sun as it strikes your property. Once you have an idea of what is sunny and what is shady, then you can orient your deck accordingly. Of course you can probably put a deck on any exposure and then combat the weather with overhangs and what-have-you, but this is hardly a wise course of action. A deck should be a deck and not a built-up outside shelter.

65. This small deck off the porch is a link between house and garden and serves its purpose well. Container plants decorate the deck to furnish a needed vertical accent. (*Photo courtesy Western Wood Products*)

Many times it is difficult to decide how large the deck should be, but there is an easy rule: make it three-fourths as large as the room it adjoins and it will always be in scale to the rest of the house. A 16-by-20-foot living room would accommodate a 12-by-16-foot deck very well and look handsome.

CONSTRUCTION

Typical construction of a low-level deck is usually posts on footings or piers. The footing anchors the decks to the site and keeps lumber from contact with the soil. Footings must extend below the frost line because

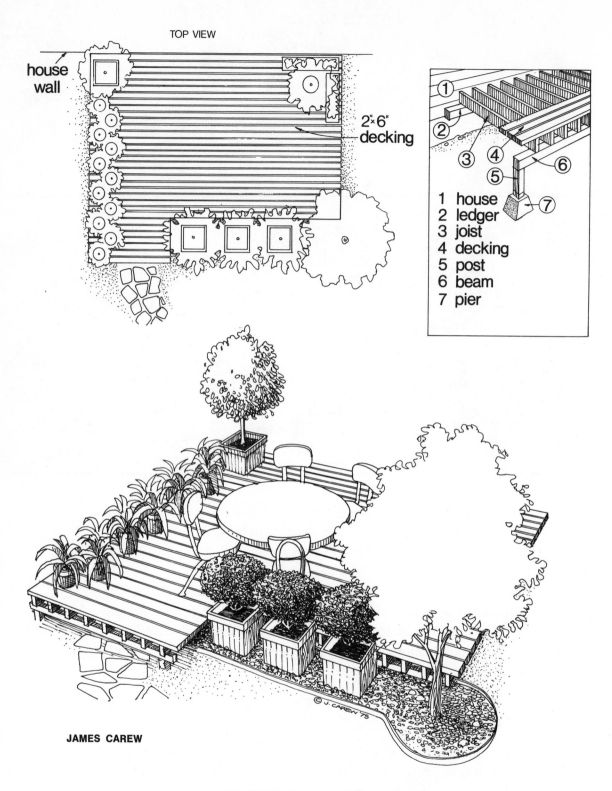

TOP VIEW

house
wall

2"x6"
decking

1 house
2 ledger
3 joist
4 decking
5 post
6 beam
7 pier

© J. CAREW 75

JAMES CAREW

Wood Decking

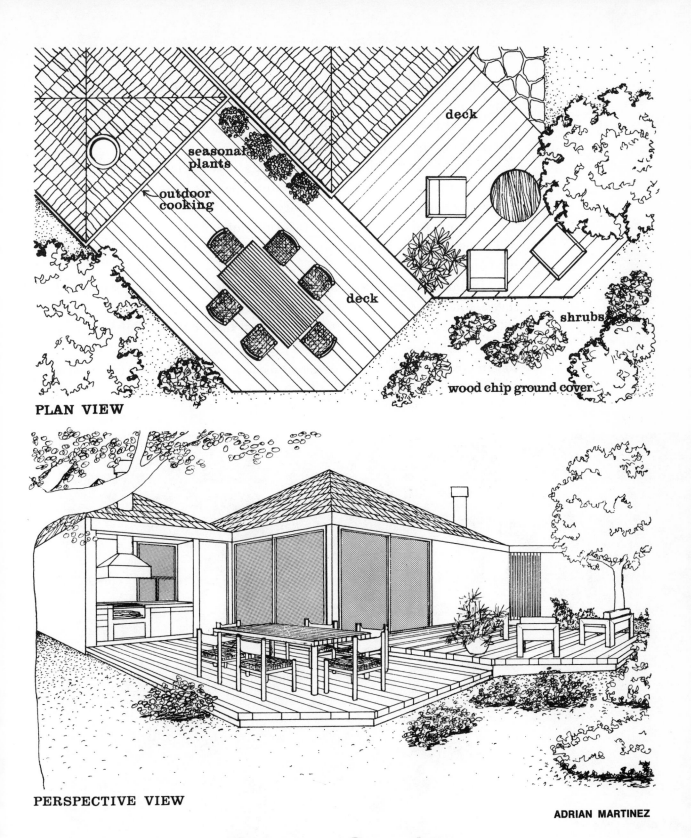

PLAN VIEW

seasonal plants

outdoor cooking

deck

deck

shrubs

wood chip ground cover

PERSPECTIVE VIEW

ADRIAN MARTINEZ

Deck Garden

water in the concrete will crack the footing when it freezes. Depending on your location you can use precast footings obtained from suppliers or concrete blocks for small ground-level decks. You can cast your own footings and piers but this is difficult work.

For building the hillside deck, footings must extend at least 30 inches below grade and be a foot or more across. These footings should contain steel reinforcing bars to hold the weight of the deck.

Footings for decks must be placed absolutely level in position so there will be no tilt to the structure. Ideally the deck should be almost level with the house floor.

To build a deck, measure and then outline the area with string and stakes. Find your first corner-post locations and put a stake in place; then with nylon string run a line to the next post hole location. Put in a stake

66. An expansive deck off the recreation room is made of 2-by-4 western wood and serves as an extension of both kitchen and recreation room to combine indoor-outdoor living. (*Photo courtesy Western Wood Products*)

67. For visual appeal this deck was designed in an arc and the results are pleasing. The sweeping curve is graceful and handsome in the garden. (*Photo by Ken Molino*)

and continue until all corners have stakes. Once you have your post hole locations, with a post-hole digger or a shovel dig down at least 20 inches (check local building offices to determine frost lines). Dig to the appropriate depth and set the footings in place.

The 4-by-4-inch post is the most-used support for ground-level decks; it bears a load weight of 8,000 pounds up to a height of 8 feet. For hillside construction where there are heavier loads, you will need substantially heavier posts—6 by 6s or perhaps even 8 by 8s. (Local building departments will advise you or your lumber house can supply this information.)

Be sure to get post heights accurate. The substructure must be level, even, and stable to support the horizontal platform with ease. To do this mark a line on the house wall that will be flush with the top of the deck surface. Measure down the thickness of the decking you are going to use

68. A basic rectangular deck of Douglas 2 by 4s has considerable design impact. The deck is actually on a garage roof; sections lift up for roof maintenance. (*Photo courtesy Western Wood Products*)

and then add the thickness of the joists to find the top of the ledger height.

To set posts in place align them so they are absolutely straight; use a carpenter's level. Now run a line from the ledger to the post and mark it. From that mark, subtract the depth of the support beam and make a new mark. Now take down the post and cut off the excess.

To prevent vertical movement of the deck crossbracing will be needed. Heavy-duty post connectors can be used between post and beam.

Beams can be nailed to posts by toenailing or with strap metal which comes in L-shaped, T-shaped, or straight pieces. Joists that will run lengthwise can be placed on top of the beams or attached flush with their tops.

Usual deck construction follows these steps:

1. Establish the location of the footing (as described).

2. Dig holes to proper depths and locate the marker lines.

3. Place the pier forms in position and level them with each other, using a line level.

4. Establish the desired level of the deck and measure down the depth of the decking plus the joists. Mark the ledger and secure to the stud, starting at the center.

5. After determining the heights, set the posts and check for plumb, using a carpenter's level on two sides.

6. With a piece of scrap lumber set on the posts, check to make sure all the parts in the row are on an even plane.

7. Check the level between the ledger and the beam to see that they are flush. Do this with a measuring tape or string.

69. This T-shaped deck off a living room is a favorite place for entertaining. The bench of 2-by-4 Douglas fir acts both as a railing and sitting area. (*Photo courtesy Western Wood Products*)

8. Secure the post to the connector.

9. Place the beam on the post and secure it by toenailing it in place.

10. Use the house wall as the base point to assure decking will be true. Be sure first the board is a straight line.

11. Nail the boards in place, using a spacer (a block of wood) between each board to assure even spaces.

Decking boards are 2 by 6 inches or 2 by 4 inches set with uniform space between each board nailed on joists, the joists in turn nailed to beams, and the beams attached to posts on piers. These are the essential steps of all deck building and can be adapted to other typical designs.

70. A step-down deck is used here to break a large expanse and works very well. The accent tree makes this handsome deck an especially pleasing area. (*Photo courtesy California Redwood Association*)

71. This completely wooden deck has many functions—as an entertaining area or a place to relax. The design is simple yet functional. (*Photo courtesy Western Wood Products*)

7. Walks and Paths

To enjoy your garden, you must be able to get from one place to another easily, so paths and walks are necessary and they are more important than you may think. Plan convenient routes for reaching flower beds and the patio from the house or from different parts of the grounds. The building of paths and walks is simple.

PLANNING

Paths and walks that are part of the total landscape plan are charming; as afterthoughts they usually appear incongruous to the scheme of things. Position paths so they give you full access to all parts of your garden; a secluded spot in back of the house is wasted if you cannot get to it. A path or walk leading to this area opens up the space for many kinds of gardens—a fern garden, a cutting garden, or even a vegetable patch.

Use some flair in planning paths. (By the way, a path is defined as a natural trail with gravel or cinder on earth; a walk is a paved surface.) The path should be not only a way of getting from one place to another but also a decorative feature. It can be a subtle turn and graceful curve to accent an area, to frame a flower bed, or to lead the eye to a garden feature. It can be an attractive pattern to break the monotony of a large area, or it can be a finely detailed ornate path with colorful tile.

The construction of the path is important, too—its suitability to the site and use, its cost, and the question of its upkeep.

Paths—walks, too—should have a beginning and lead to a point of interest or connect with other paths. Make the path broad—at least 3 to 5 feet wide—for two people to walk abreast. Narrow paths create a traffic

72. In a large garden area, a path of concrete steppingstones adds just the right amount of color and design to the landscape. (*Photo by Molly Adams*)

problem. The width should have some relation to the length; good proportion is important.

BRICK AND CONCRETE
FOR PATHS AND WALKS

For walks, brick is excellent because it harmonizes well with nearly every outdoor situation and is easy to install. It can be laid on a well-tamped-down sand or cinder base or be set in mortar. There are many patterns to add an interesting note to the garden, and brick lasts for years.

Concrete is another material for walks. It is durable, but it is not always suitable because of its sterile gray color. And even though it lasts for

73. Concrete aggregate blocks create the path to the swimming pool; they are neat and unobtrusive and blend well with the grass area. (*Photo by Ken Molino*)

74. To provide access to the patio area, rounds of wood are most effective. They are visually pleasing and provide drama in the outdoor scene. (*Photo courtesy Western Wood Products*)

75. Simple concrete paving works well as the path to this house; it is natural and blends well with the greenery. (*Photo courtesy Theodore Brickman, Landscape Architect*)

years, it is difficult to install. On the other hand, concrete steppingstones are decorative and easy to put in place; so are patio pavers and patio blocks. Investigate local building-supply yards carefully because there are many new types of steppingstones for walks.

Walks need layout, excavation, and subsurfacing. A depth of 6 to 8 inches will accommodate a gravel base of 2 to 4 inches and poured concrete to 3 to 4 inches.

When you use gravel on cinders or crushed rock for paths dig down at least 2 to 3 inches and install the material. For a durable path first install a 1-inch base of packed rock such as decomposed granite. For the top layer use ½-to-¾-inch gravel. Smaller stones sink into the gravel and larger stones are uncomfortable to walk on. Apply stones in thin layers—½ inch is best —rake, moisten, and then install another layer, and so on.

LOOSE-FILL MATERIALS

Ground bark, gravel, cinder, or grass are commonly used for paths but gravel has to be replaced every year or so. And grass, while lovely, has limi-

76. Concrete blocks in a random design are used as a path to a contemporary home; they are in character with the house and in tune with the complete landscape plan. (*Photo courtesy Theodore Brickman, Landscape Architect*)

77. Serpentine concrete paths are the network through a lovely city garden; note that all parts of the garden can easily be reached. (*Photo by Pat Matsumoto*)

tations if there is heavy foot traffic. Before you choose a material for a path or walk determine the following:

1. Will the surfacing have a pleasant feel underfoot?

2. Will the color, pattern, and texture blend with other surfaces?

3. Will it withstand weather?

4. Will it last a long time?

5. Will it be easy to clean?

6. Will you be able to install it yourself?

7. Will weeds grow through it?

78. Here, a rubble path leads to the garden. In a natural landscape such as this the rubble rockwork blends well as a natural component. (*Photo by Roger Scharmer*)

79. Some steppingstones and a bridge of wood provide access to this totally charming natural garden; a pleasant picture. (*Photo by Molly Adams*)

80. When there is a large garden area, steps do much to break the expanse and create levels so necessary in such a situation. The total effect is charming. (*Photo by Molly Adams*)

STEPS

Where there is a change of levels in the garden don't miss the opportunity of using steps. They break the monotony of a landscape with graceful and sweeping lines and add visual interest. They do not have to be straight or precise unless you have a very formal garden.

There are many arrangements for steps but shape suggestions are difficult. It depends on the landscape plan. In general a straight flight of steps

OPPOSITE
81. A masonry stairway is just what this informal garden needed and it becomes the accent of the landscape, both natural and useful. (*Photo by Joyce R. Wilson*)

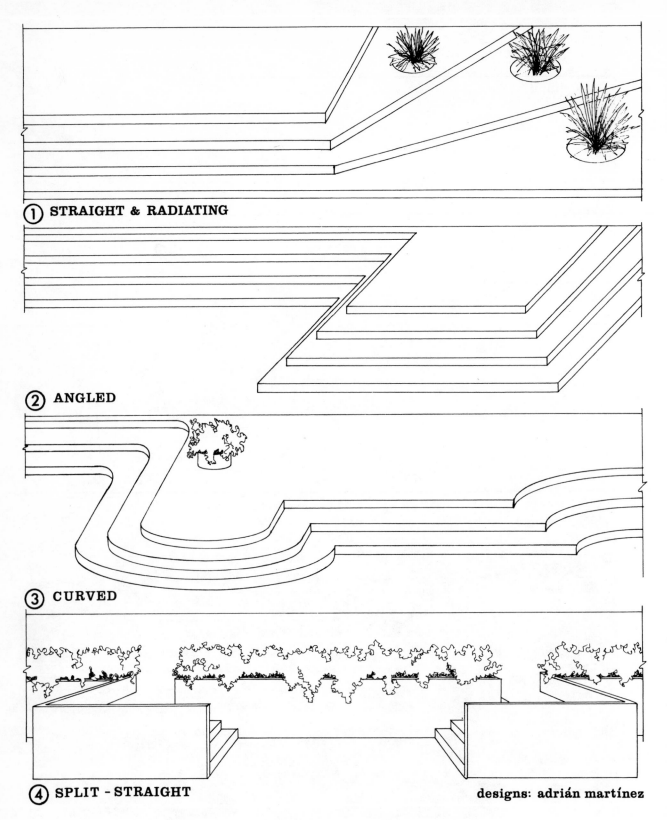

① STRAIGHT & RADIATING

② ANGLED

③ CURVED

④ SPLIT - STRAIGHT

designs: adrián martínez

Step Arrangements

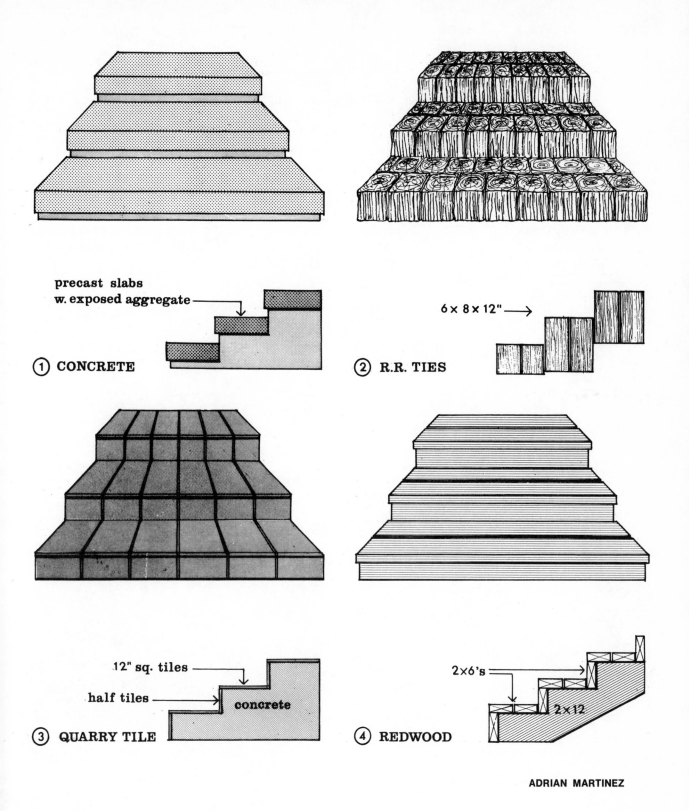

precast slabs
w. exposed aggregate

6 × 8 × 12"→

① CONCRETE

② R.R. TIES

12" sq. tiles

half tiles

concrete

2×6's

2×12

③ QUARRY TILE

④ REDWOOD

ADRIAN MARTINEZ

Types of Steps

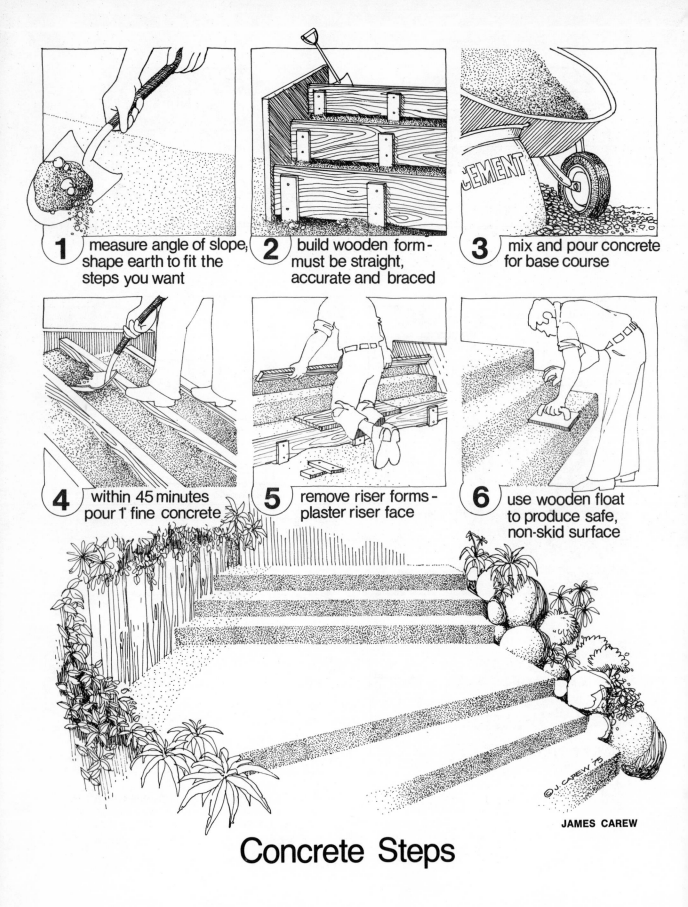

1 measure angle of slope, shape earth to fit the steps you want

2 build wooden form - must be straight, accurate and braced

3 mix and pour concrete for base course

4 within 45 minutes pour 1" fine concrete

5 remove riser forms - plaster riser face

6 use wooden float to produce safe, non-skid surface

JAMES CAREW

Concrete Steps

82. Only one simple wooden step was used on this patio and it does the job. It complements the concrete work and provides a visual accent. (*Photo courtesy California Association of Nurserymen*)

is hardly pleasing; turns and angles with wide or low treads are more graceful and effective in the landscape. Generally, a 14-inch tread with a rise of about 6 inches is fine for garden steps.

If there is a long flight of steps, install a landing between them with perhaps a change of direction to break the monotony of a long step area.

There is a vast array of materials for steps—concrete or pieces of brick, precast slabs, logs or railroad ties, to mention a few. As a rule, steps do not require perfect detailing because garden plants can be used to soften the rough edges.

8. Outdoor Lighting

While garden lighting is not inexpensive, it is well worth the expenditure because it allows you to use the garden at night. (An evening stroll in the garden is solace for the soul.) And lighting is a safety factor. It deters prowlers. Knowing how to light the garden and what is available in lighting fixtures are necessary to do an intelligent job in garden lighting. Lights for specific areas need not be expensive.

While lighting itself is not considered an outdoor building project, too many gardens are not lighted at night and thus are only part-time areas. Lights make the garden or patio a full-time place, so this information is included here.

LIGHTING SYSTEMS

The traditional type of landscape lighting is a standard 120-volt system. It furnishes bright light and comes in a wide selection of fixtures. It is probably the most dependable but also the most expensive type of lighting. For small gardens, however, it is not exorbitant. Use chemically coated wires buried in the ground in trenches at least 18 inches deep. Outlet boxes are necessary and usually trench cable must be grounded. These are jobs for professional electricians.

The low-voltage (L-v) system is more a do-it-yourself project and it is a safe, good way to light a garden if all rules are followed. You can install this yourself because even if you accidentally cut a cable there will be no heavy shock. The guts of the L-v system is a transformer; you can attach it to a wall and then plug it into any outdoor outlet. The transformer re-

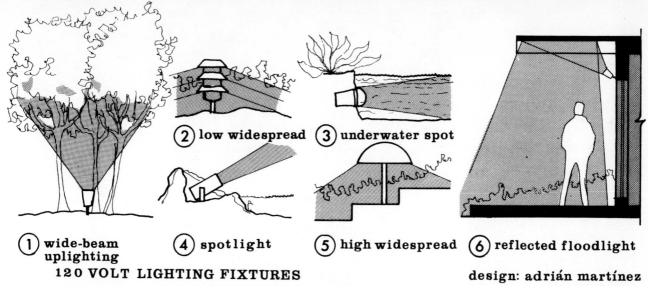

① wide-beam uplighting
② low widespread
③ underwater spot
④ spotlight
⑤ high widespread
⑥ reflected floodlight

120 VOLT LIGHTING FIXTURES

design: adrián martínez

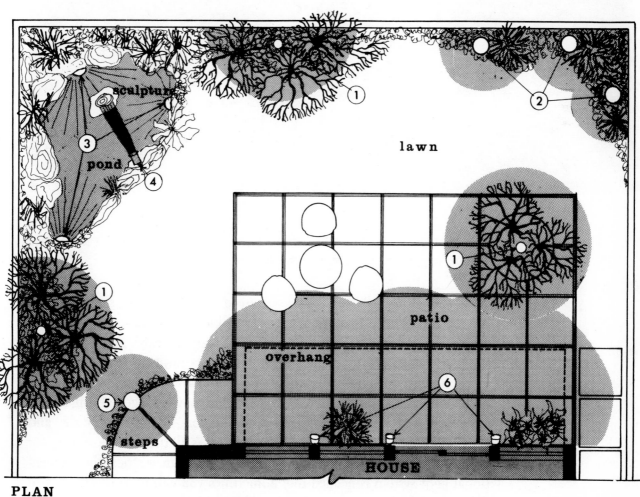

sculpture

pond

lawn

patio

overhang

steps

HOUSE

PLAN

Landscape Lighting

83. Outdoor lighting makes gardens 24-hour places; this lovely patio is beautifully lighted. Canopy fixtures outline the patio area and the fountain is exquisitely illuminated. (*Photo courtesy General Electric Company*)

duces the normal 120-volt house system to 12 volts. Unlike standard electric cable that must be buried deep, the cables for the L-v system require only a 2-inch depth below ground level. Wedge the earth apart with your shoe or spade, put the cables in place, and tamp down the soil.

The system comes in a variety of kits with transformer, but generally has 6 or 8 fixtures and about 100 feet of cable. Low-voltage lighting is subdued light that is fine for decorative effects along flower beds, walls, and for safety lighting along paths. Generally, this is all that is necessary in the average garden. If you have large patio or game areas, then the conventional light system is needed too. Sometimes you will need several kits to light all outdoor areas properly. Use a kit—with 6 fixtures—for each area— patio, pool—with a separate system for each. Then it is simple to control areas where light is or is not needed.

FUNCTIONS OF LIGHTING

Lighting provides safety as well as a decorative accent in the garden. Light all steps and paths and dramatize special trees or accents in the garden with lights. Here are some helpful hints for lighting your property:

Silhouette lighting. This is lighting from above to create halos below and light coming from below to outline plants. The light source is directed at a wall, fence, or shrubbery behind the object with little light at the front.

Etch lighting. Etched lighting is used to emphasize surface objects. The light source at a distance of 4 to 10 inches is aimed parallel to the surface of the object.

Contour lighting. This lighting is used for creating depth and three-dimensional character in a subject. It is light aimed at an object from several directions with more light from one side than the other.

84. Trees become pieces of sculpture with proper lighting. Here two floodlamps do the job. (*Photo courtesy General Electric Company*)

85. Simple fixtures at the tops of the windows illuminate a charming garden spot for night-time viewing. It is dramatic and handsome. (*Photo courtesy General Electric Company*)

Color lights. These are used for drama and too much can be unattractive. Use with discretion.

RULES TO FOLLOW IN LIGHTING

Always place lights so they are concealed from view.

Do not use too many lights.

Create an interplay of light and shadow.

Keep illumination at different intensity levels throughout the yard.

Do not light a subject head-on.

Place fixtures on two sides of an object rather than one side.

Use walls and fences as reflecting surfaces.

Never aim fixtures at neighbors' property.

BULBS AND FIXTURES

The main lighting lamp for outdoors is the PAR lamp. It is not affected by ice, snow, water, or fluctuating temperatures. This sealed unit, usually mushroom-shaped, comes in flood or spotlight designs. The wattages are 75, 100, and 150. Also offered are very-high-intensity PAR lamps of 200 and 300 watts. All outdoor lamps should be installed in fixtures with waterproof sockets (available at dealers).

Some people use common household lamps outdoors but this is generally not a good practice. You can use 10- or 15-watt indoor lamps out-

86. Lighting for safety's sake makes sense; this home is properly illuminated. Note the attractive lamps at the corner of the garage and a lamp at the entrance. (*Photo courtesy General Electric Company*)

87. Floodlamps illuminate this patio and other outdoor lighting accents the garden area beyond. (*Photo courtesy Westinghouse Electric Company*)

88. Flower beds take on added dimension with two simple canopy fixtures. (*Photo courtesy Westinghouse Electric Company*)

89. For safety, stairs in gardens should always be illuminated; the effect is handsome as well. (*Photo courtesy Westinghouse Electric Company*)

doors but any brighter light would need protection from the weather. Mercury vapor lamps—with very high light intensity—and cold quartz lamps are also available but usually are too bright for most garden areas.

Fixtures for outdoor lighting come in a variety of designs but the one you will work with the most is the bullet-type fixture. This fixture directs the light to the object, is inexpensive, and comes in several finishes. Canopy fixtures for flower beds and stairs are also available and very ornamental fixtures that simulate leaves or flowers can also be used if you desire. Some fixtures are portable, mounted on metal spikes that stick into the ground, while others are for permanent installation on house walls or fences.

Your local electrical-supply dealer will have a wide variety of fixtures and lamps and it's wise to shop a little before you buy, not only for price but for styles and designs.

If you would rather not buy commercial fixtures you can make your own lighting units using plywood (see drawing opposite).

90. The lighting in the overhang of the house illuminates the pool area and the pool itself is lighted for safety and beauty. (*Photo courtesy General Electric Company*)

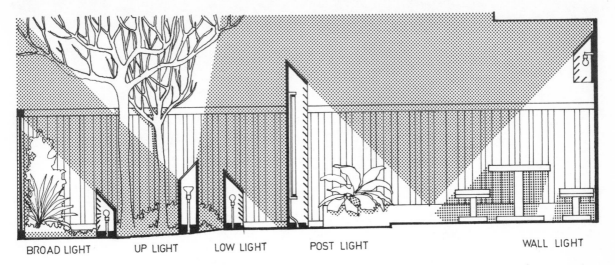

BROAD LIGHT   UP LIGHT   LOW LIGHT   POST LIGHT   WALL LIGHT

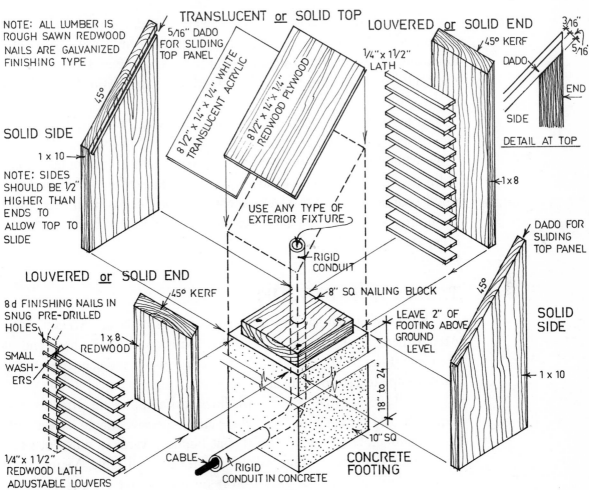

NOTE: ALL LUMBER IS
ROUGH SAWN REDWOOD
NAILS ARE GALVANIZED
FINISHING TYPE

TRANSLUCENT or SOLID TOP

5/16" DADO
FOR SLIDING
TOP PANEL

8 1/2" x 14" x 1/4" WHITE
TRANSLUCENT ACRYLIC

8 1/2" x 14" x 1/4"
REDWOOD PLYWOOD

LOUVERED or SOLID END

1/4" x 1 1/2"
LATH

45°

SOLID SIDE

1 x 10

NOTE: SIDES
SHOULD BE 1/2"
HIGHER THAN
ENDS TO
ALLOW TOP TO
SLIDE

45° KERF

DADO

END

SIDE

3/16"

5/16"

DETAIL AT TOP

1 x 8

USE ANY TYPE OF
EXTERIOR FIXTURE

RIGID
CONDUIT

8" SQ NAILING BLOCK

LEAVE 2" OF
FOOTING ABOVE
GROUND
LEVEL

DADO FOR
SLIDING
TOP PANEL

45°

SOLID
SIDE

1 x 10

18" to 24"

10" SQ

CONCRETE
FOOTING

LOUVERED or SOLID END

8 d FINISHING NAILS IN
SNUG PRE-DRILLED
HOLES

SMALL
WASH-
ERS

45° KERF

1 x 8
REDWOOD

1/4" x 1 1/2"
REDWOOD LATH
ADJUSTABLE LOUVERS

CABLE

RIGID
CONDUIT IN CONCRETE

Outdoor Lighting Units

design/drawing : Adrián Martínez

9. Garden Furniture

Garden furniture adds interest to a garden and of course makes it an all-purpose outdoor area. You can make your own furniture and decorations and these generally will be superior to those you might buy. Benches and tables, arches and trellises, plant stands and light fixtures, are all part of the garden scene.

Many outdoor decorations are built with wood, but bricks, concrete blocks, and flat glass (available at building-supply yards) are also used. Salvage items can be put to work too. Hatch covers are ideal for table tops, railroad ties covered with a pane of glass make an excellent table, and redwood boards on concrete blocks become a fine bench. Birdbaths, small sculptures, and concrete panels cast in sand to decorate fences are some other ideas.

TABLES AND BENCHES

For a simple garden bench, concrete blocks make an excellent base. Attach them to any masonry patio floor with epoxy solutions found at hardware stores. Angle irons bolted to a redwood top and cemented to the block complete a sturdy bench.

Small accent tables made of tile flues or drainpipes are attractive and require hardly any construction. This is an inexpensive way to have a table in the garden. The tiles are available at builders' yards in different sizes. An 18-inch diameter is quite satisfactory for a small table. Merely set a pane of glass (available at glass stores) on the tile flue for a table. Small drainpipes 5 inches in diameter can be grouped together in a honeycomb pattern and covered with glass for another unique table. A simple, elegant bench made with 2 by 4s is shown in the drawing.

142

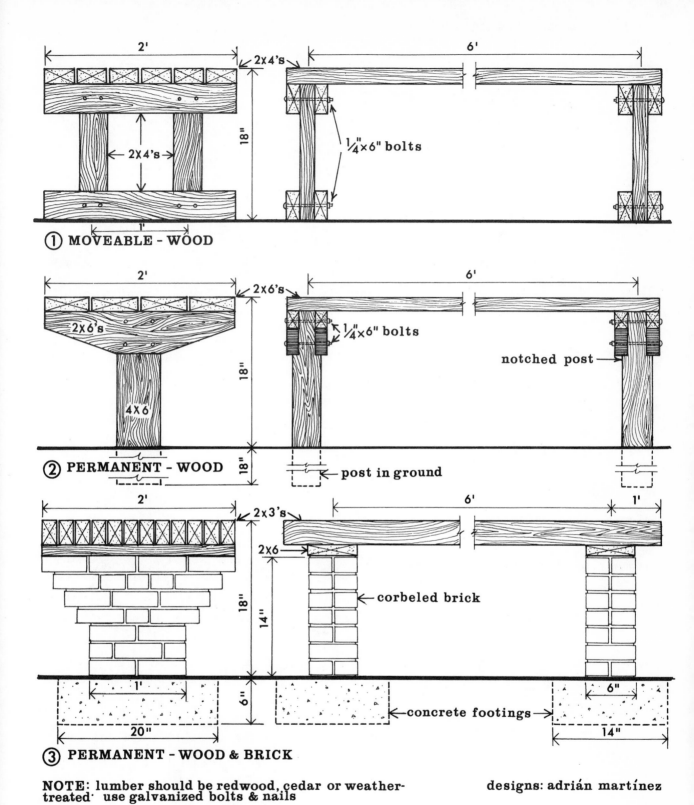

① **MOVEABLE - WOOD**

2'
2x4's
2x4's
18"
1"
6'
¼"x6" bolts

② **PERMANENT - WOOD**

2'
2x6's
2x6's
4x6
18"
18"
6'
¼"x6" bolts
notched post
post in ground

③ **PERMANENT - WOOD & BRICK**

2'
2x3's
2x6
18"
14"
1'
6"
20"
6'
1'
corbeled brick
concrete footings
6"
14"

NOTE: lumber should be redwood, cedar or weather-treated· use galvanized bolts & nails

designs: adrián martínez

Bench Designs

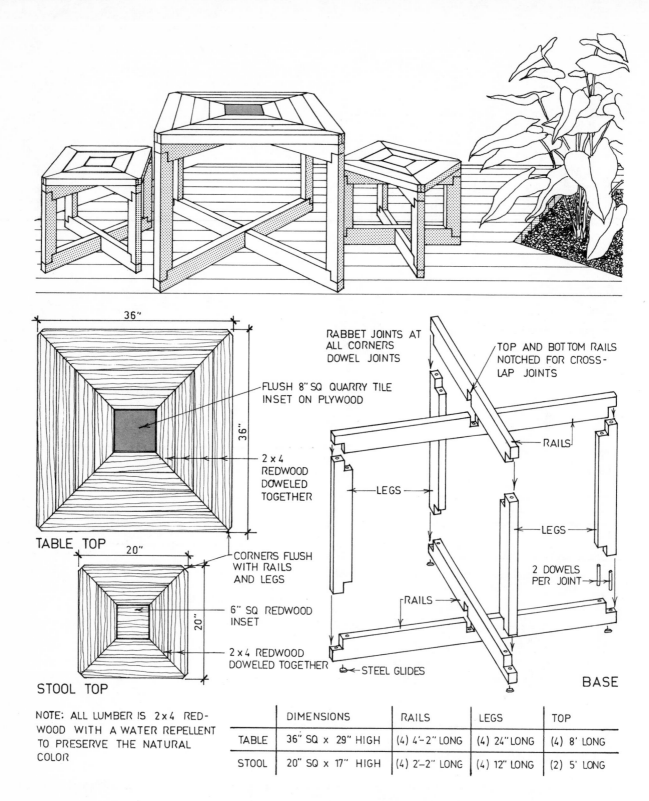

36"

36"

FLUSH 8" SQ QUARRY TILE
INSET ON PLYWOOD

2 x 4
REDWOOD
DOWELED
TOGETHER

TABLE TOP

20"

20"

CORNERS FLUSH
WITH RAILS
AND LEGS

6" SQ REDWOOD
INSET

2 x 4 REDWOOD
DOWELED TOGETHER

STOOL TOP

RABBET JOINTS AT
ALL CORNERS
DOWEL JOINTS

TOP AND BOTTOM RAILS
NOTCHED FOR CROSS-
LAP JOINTS

RAILS

LEGS

LEGS

2 DOWELS
PER JOINT

RAILS

STEEL GLIDES

BASE

NOTE: ALL LUMBER IS 2x4 RED-
WOOD WITH A WATER REPELLENT
TO PRESERVE THE NATURAL
COLOR

	DIMENSIONS	RAILS	LEGS	TOP
TABLE	36" SQ x 29" HIGH	(4) 4'-2" LONG	(4) 24" LONG	(4) 8' LONG
STOOL	20" SQ x 17" HIGH	(4) 2'-2" LONG	(4) 12" LONG	(2) 5' LONG

Outdoor Table and Stools

design/drawing: Adrián Martínez

If you want to mix crafts with construction, set mosaic pieces in mortar on a plywood base and trim with a wooden molding for an attractive piece. Art stores have special kits containing mosaics and epoxies.

A bench in the garden or patio is more than a place to rest; it is a decorative feature too. A simple bench can be free-standing or part of the patio design and can be built inexpensively. Benches can border an area and act as a frame or at different levels break the monotony of a landscape. One end of the bench can be for seating, the other a display platform for container plants.

The design of the bench in all likelihood will not have a back to obstruct a view. Although an ideal place for a bench is along a wall or a fence, it can also be an island or frame a tree or a piece of sculpture. Even a cantilevered bench is not difficult to make. For color, benches can be covered with bright, weather-resistant fabrics.

Make benches 15 to 18 inches high (depending on their use) if they are to be for sitting; for sunbathing, an 8-inch height is ideal. The width can be from 24 to 28 inches depending on its use. A simple bench is made from 2-inch redwood stocks for the top, spaced about ½ inch apart and set on concrete blocks 3 feet apart.

Another sturdy bench can be made from an 8-foot board. Cut two 12-inch lengths, and you have both legs and the top with a 2 by 4 board for the leg brace. The legs are secured to the brace, and then the three-piece bottom section is toenailed to the top.

A slat bench is another idea. Use 1-by-2-inch lumber set on edge spaced 1 inch apart in a wooden frame. Bolt the top section to U-shaped straps sunk in 4-by-8-by-16-inch blocks.

BENCH DESIGNS

There are several designs for benches, and these are some general rules to follow:

1. Redwood and cedar are the best woods to use. They weather well and usually need no preservatives. Select finished grade for the top. Lower grade, such as rough finish, is fine for the lower parts of the bench.

2. Where strong support is needed, use 2-inch-thick lumber for bench tops. Leave ½-inch spaces between the boards for water drainage.

91. This barbecue pit doubles as a table; the wooden benches add to the attractive unit. (*Photo courtesy Western Wood Products*)

92. The pit is made of concrete block.
(*Photo courtesy Western Wood Products*)

93. Close-up of wood detailing.
(*Photo courtesy Western Wood Products*)

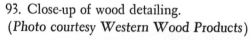

94. Side construction.
(*Photo courtesy Western Wood Products*)

95. Corner construction.
(*Photo courtesy Western Wood Products*)

3. To prevent the wood from being stained by nails and screws, use galvanized nonrusting nails and screws.

4. Make the bench legs sturdy enough to support weight but keep the legs in scale with the design.

5. Space legs about 3 to 5 feet apart for large benches, closer together for smaller ones.

6. To finish redwood or cedar, use a water-repellent product and then a sealer—or paint the benches.

MATERIALS NEEDED

For garden furniture use first-quality wood; kiln-dried or heartwood is suggested because you want smooth surfaces without knotholes or other

96. These simple wooden benches are easy to make, look handsome, and define the perimeter of the deck. (*Photo courtesy Western Wood Products*)

blemishes. Use 2-inch-thick boards or 1-inch plywood on most garden furniture and remember that the wider the wood, the more apt it is to warp. Kiln-dried wood, as suggested, minimizes warping.

For furniture building you will need: hammers, electric handsaw, drills, nails, bolts, screws, and wood epoxies. To prevent staining use rustproof nails, and of course, for waterproofing, a suitable epoxy.

97. An L-shaped wooden platform doubles as a sitting area. (*Photo courtesy California Redwood Association*)

98. This sitting deck transforms part of the yard into a cozy garden spot. The long benches are made of 2-by-6-inch boards on 4-by-4-inch posts. (*Photo courtesy Western Wood Products*)

99. Close-up photos of corner construction of redwood slat bench. (*Photo courtesy California Redwood Association*)

PLANT STANDS

Plant stands are not necessarily tables although they can double as tables too. Usually a plant stand is a simple redwood structure that is easily made. It elevates plants off the patio and gives them another dimension. Several stands at varying heights create a lovely pot garden. The drawing for plant stands will show you how to make them and you can of course vary the design somewhat to fit your tastes. In essence, plant stands should be neither too large nor too small. Large ones look clumsy and obstructive in the garden and small ones are out of scale to the great outdoors. A good size is 18 by 18 inches square with a slatted 24-inch top.

PORTABLE GARDEN STOOL

The portable garden stool shown in the drawing opposite offers an easy way to garden while seated. For elderly people or those with back problems

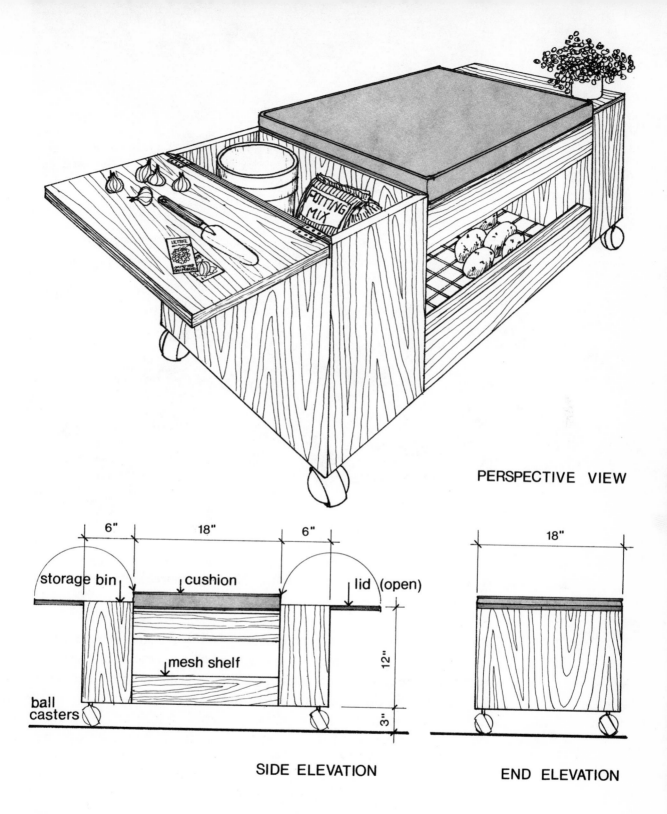

PERSPECTIVE VIEW

6"   18"   6"

storage bin   cushion   lid (open)

mesh shelf

12"

ball casters

3"

SIDE ELEVATION

18"

END ELEVATION

Portable Garden Stool

DESIGN: ADRIÁN MARTÍNEZ

100. The railing, bench, and plant container are homemade of redwood. Architectural in design and handsome, this is a pleasing arrangement for garden decor. (*Photo courtesy California Redwood Association*)

this little stool is worth its weight in gold. While the stool is a place to sit, it is also a place to keep tools so you have everything in one place when you need it. If you do not want to make the stool yourself, ask a carpenter to do it, following the directions in the drawing.

CANVAS SWING

This is for the lazy gardener, and what a joy it is after working in the garden to relax in this swing! The structure is easily made from 2-by-4-inch redwood and pipes. The fittings used to attach the swing to a stable structure are eye bolts. The cost of the canvas swing should not be over $50.

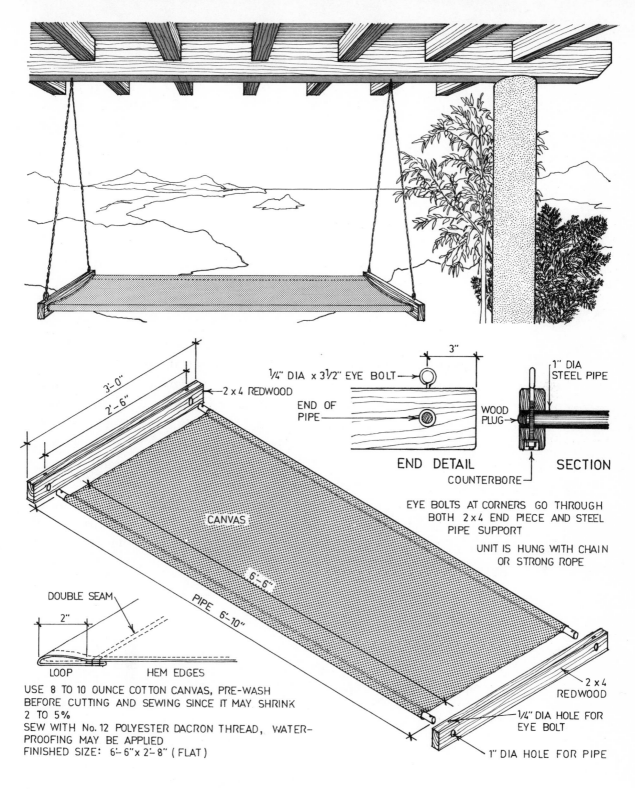

3'-0"

2'-6"

2 x 4 REDWOOD

¼" DIA x 3½" EYE BOLT

3"

END OF PIPE

1" DIA STEEL PIPE

WOOD PLUG

CANVAS

END DETAIL

COUNTERBORE

SECTION

6'-6"

PIPE 6'-10"

EYE BOLTS AT CORNERS GO THROUGH BOTH 2 x 4 END PIECE AND STEEL PIPE SUPPORT

UNIT IS HUNG WITH CHAIN OR STRONG ROPE

DOUBLE SEAM

2"

LOOP   HEM EDGES

USE 8 TO 10 OUNCE COTTON CANVAS, PRE-WASH BEFORE CUTTING AND SEWING SINCE IT MAY SHRINK 2 TO 5%
SEW WITH No.12 POLYESTER DACRON THREAD, WATER-PROOFING MAY BE APPLIED
FINISHED SIZE: 6'-6"x 2'-8" (FLAT)

2 x 4 REDWOOD

¼" DIA HOLE FOR EYE BOLT

1" DIA HOLE FOR PIPE

Canvas Lounge Swing

design/drawing: Adrián Martínez

10. Make Your Own Containers

The nice thing about building your own containers is that you fit planters into appropriate areas; custom detailing always looks best. Hanging baskets take little time to make, are easily assembled, and are inexpensive; they are lovely hanging decorations for porches and patios. They may be permanent or a modular type that you can move around. Boxes for trees should be cube-shaped—deep; other planter boxes for bedding plants are generally long and narrow, say about 36 inches wide. You can make small boxes or large ones. Windowboxes are other containers that can be used in windows to complement other garden plants. If you are handy and like working with pottery you can make concrete tubs and urns for plants. These add elegance to gardens and are not generally available in stores.

WOOD

Wood is the most durable and popular material for tubs and boxes. It lasts a long time, is easy to work with, and the natural finish looks well on patios and terraces. Simple boxes can be made in a jiffy using four sides and a bottom of 2-by-12-inch redwood. Redwood and cedar weather beautifully over the years, and as mentioned in chapter 1 are impervious to weather; they need no protective finish. For decorative effect, they can be scored or grooved or sandblasted.

Douglas fir, a stronger wood, is best for very large boxes; say over 24 by 24 inches. Fir needs a preservative coating, and while it will not last as long outdoors—about five years—it still is satisfactory. It can be

101. Wooden planters such as these can be made with 2-by-12-inch boards; use construction-grade redwood. The boxes are simple to build; note the raised platforms under the containers to permit air to reach the bottoms of the plants. (*Photo by Matthew Barr*)

stained to give it a finished appearance or painted. Pine is a soft wood and has its use for garden containers such as small bulb boxes on planting beds. For maximum longevity treat it with a preservative or have a galvanized metal liner made at a sheet-metal shop for the box. While the liners are expensive, they add years of life to the planters.

Nail boxes together, or for sturdier construction use glue and screws. Use brass screws and good-quality wood epoxy. One-inch lumber is fine for most small boxes, but for larger containers use a 2-inch stock.

When you make your own containers you can have flared or tapered sides—ideal boxes for dish gardens, annuals, almost any planting. You can also make wall-mounted planters using a standard concrete tub or pot anchored to a redwood shelf with supporting brackets. These units are especially good against fences.

planters
must have
adequate
drainage

①drill holes
at planter base

②add
drainage
stones

fasten boards with nails
and/or miter joints

use miter box
for cutting angles

JAMES CAREW

Modular Planters

102. This decorative planter was custom made to fit a specific area; the outside detailing is handsome and the box solidly constructed for years of use. (*Photo courtesy California Redwood Association*)

A simple rectangular box 3 inches deep made from 1-inch redwood is ideal for small succulents, flowering bulbs, and other low-growing plants. I use brass screws to fasten the sides; ¾-inch stock for the bottom; and 1-by-1-inch platform legs at each corner. These are nailed in place. After the box is finished drill ¼-inch drain holes in the bottom.

A cube design for a planter is neat and simple and can be used in many areas of the garden for seasonal color when brimming with plants. A unique square box is shown in the drawing on p. 159 made of 2 by 4s. For a 12-inch box, 1 by 12s are best. Build it the same way as a standard planter. For larger containers, say a small tree or a shrub, use 2-by-12-inch lumber.

103. Easier to make than it appears, this handsome planter relies on the outside motif of wood bars to provide beauty. Be sure to drill drain holes in the bottom of homemade containers. (*Photo courtesy Western Wood Products*)

1 trim boards to size using miter box for cutting angles

2 drill drainage holes

3 assemble with nails

4 cut 6″ section of 4″×4″ for base support adding four 6″×10″ planks for stability

5 nail planter box to base

SIDE VIEW

TOP VIEW

JAMES CAREW

Box Planter

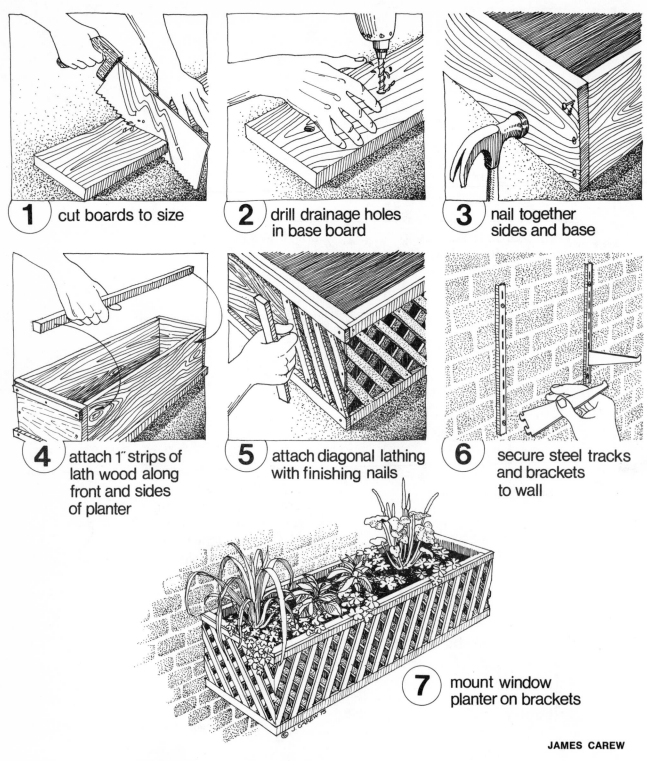

1 cut boards to size

2 drill drainage holes in base board

3 nail together sides and base

4 attach 1″ strips of lath wood along front and sides of planter

5 attach diagonal lathing with finishing nails

6 secure steel tracks and brackets to wall

7 mount window planter on brackets

JAMES CAREW

Redwood Window Planter

If you want something other than a wooden container outdoors try a sheet-metal planter box as shown in the drawing on p. 164. This box is essentially made of sheet metal (from shops) and framed with redwood. It affords a different look in the garden.

Sometimes the cube or square container is not suitable for a garden; it may be too clumsy or too angular. If such is the case, consider the tapered box. Using 2-by-14-inch redwood you can make a handsome tapered box for plants; the bottom is plywood. As with all containers drill holes in the bottom so excess water can escape.

104. Here is a galaxy of containers you can make; some are natural wood, others painted. (*Photo courtesy California Redwood Association*)

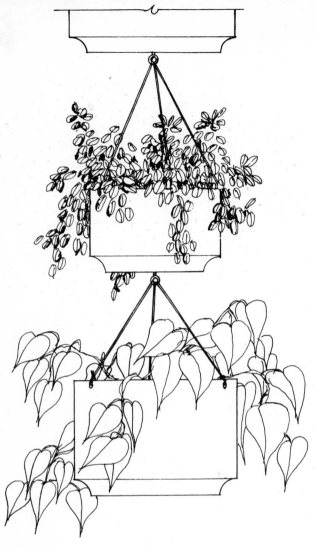

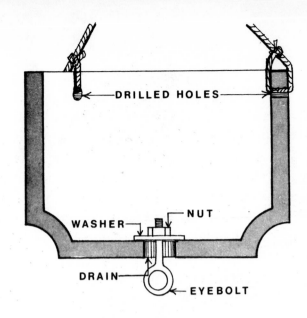

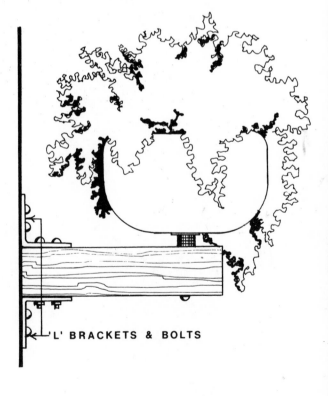

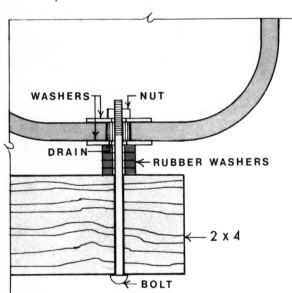

DRILLED HOLES

WASHER

NUT

DRAIN

EYEBOLT

Tiered
Hanging Planters

WASHERS

NUT

DRAIN

RUBBER WASHERS

2 x 4

BOLT

'L' BRACKETS & BOLTS

ADRIÁN MARTÍNEZ

Wall Mounted Planter

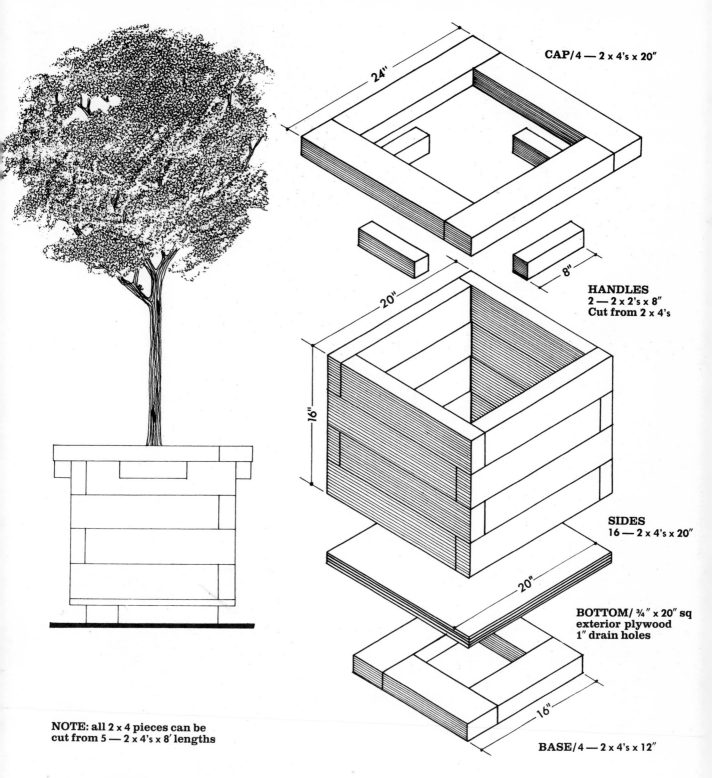

CAP/4 — 2 x 4's x 20"

24"

8"

HANDLES
2 — 2 x 2's x 8"
Cut from 2 x 4's

20"

16"

SIDES
16 — 2 x 4's x 20"

20"

BOTTOM/ ¾" x 20" sq
exterior plywood
1" drain holes

16"

BASE/4 — 2 x 4's x 12"

NOTE: all 2 x 4 pieces can be
cut from 5 — 2 x 4's x 8' lengths

ADRIAN MARTINEZ

Tree Planter Box

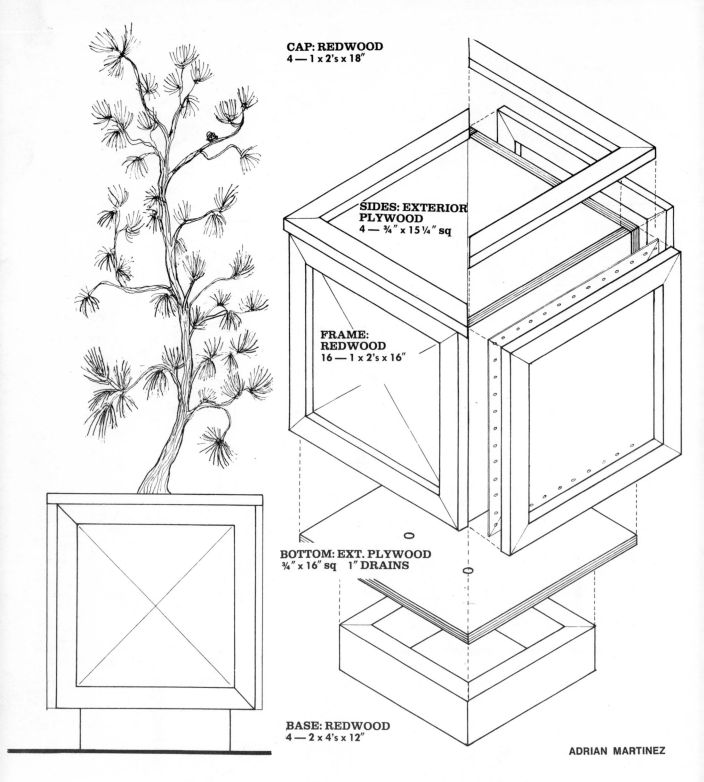

CAP: REDWOOD
4 — 1 x 2's x 18"

SIDES: EXTERIOR PLYWOOD
4 — ¾" x 15¼" sq

FRAME: REDWOOD
16 — 1 x 2's x 16"

BOTTOM: EXT. PLYWOOD
¾" x 16" sq   1" DRAINS

BASE: REDWOOD
4 — 2 x 4's x 12"

ADRIAN MARTINEZ

Sheet   Metal   Planter

105. Even one planter can add beauty to a deck or patio; this redwood box with molding does the job well. (*Photo courtesy Western Wood Products*)

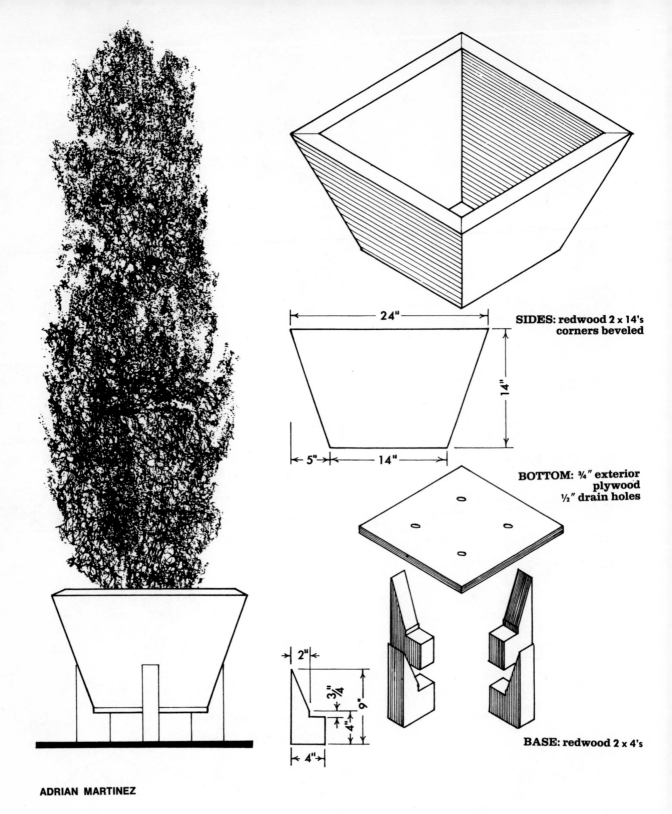

24"

14"

5" 14"

SIDES: redwood 2 x 14's
corners beveled

BOTTOM: ¾″ exterior
plywood
½″ drain holes

2"

3¾″

4"

9"

4"

BASE: redwood 2 x 4's

ADRIAN MARTINEZ

Tapered Planter Box

106. At the right is a handsome wooden planter; the shadow-box detailing makes it very attractive. (*Photo courtesy California Redwood Association*)

CONCRETE

If you want to make concrete containers be prepared for some work but the efforts are well worth the rewards. Well-crafted concrete tubs are prizes indeed. You need wood framing for the size of the box desired and a concrete mix that is fairly stiff: 3 parts cement, 1 part sand, and 2 parts pebbles. Or use Sakrete commercial mix and just add water. Pour the mix into the forms, put a presoaked standard clay pot in position, and fill in with concrete to the top of the frame. When the concrete is firm, scrub it with a wire brush, and 24 hours later strip off the wooden forms and take out the pot. Run water over the surface and scrub it with a wire brush.

Other concrete containers can be made from two cardboard cartons. Use one small enough to leave 1½ to 2 inches of space at the bottom and four sides when placed inside the other one. Pour 2 inches of concrete mix into the bottom of the first carton. Tamp down; then put the smaller carton inside. Pour and tamp the mix between the two cartons to make the walls of the planter. Cardboard forms can be removed in a day. Let the concrete dry slowly for a few days. Then, using a chisel, shape the planter. Scrub it with a wire brush and wet it down several times before using it. All sizes and shapes can be made using one of the two methods described above.

An exposed aggregate finish can be used for variation. Scrub the concrete surface with a wire brush after it has set overnight. Or, for another variation, you might want to apply integral color pigment to the concrete before it is poured. Another possibility is to add beach pebbles to the mix for a contrasting texture.

PERMANENT PLANTERS

In gardens, permanent planters of brick, wood, or concrete are often seen. They are attached to the house walls or built to fit a special place. They can be rectangular, square, triangular, or circular. Like tubs and pots, their value is largely decorative.

Outdoor planters attached to entrances or the front of a house should be in proper scale and proportion to the building. Because they cannot be removed, they should have galvanized metal liners for durability and adequate facilities for drainage. Although redwood planters are attractive in a garden, brick and stone boxes are superior in appearance.

Raised planter beds of brick look well in the landscape and have several advantages. They make it easier to tend to plants and they provide excellent drainage for them. Furthermore, the retaining walls of raised planters keep out greedy roots of nearby trees and shrubs. Also, raising the beds makes the flowers and foliage appear more attractive, bringing them closer to eye level.

To build a planter, lay out a line you want to follow on the ground and dig a trench about 15 inches deep. Make it 5 inches wider than the wall you are planning. Fill the trench with concrete—1 part cement, 3 parts sand, and 5 parts gravel. When the footing is dry, install the brick on it, using mortar and checking each brick with a mason's level to make

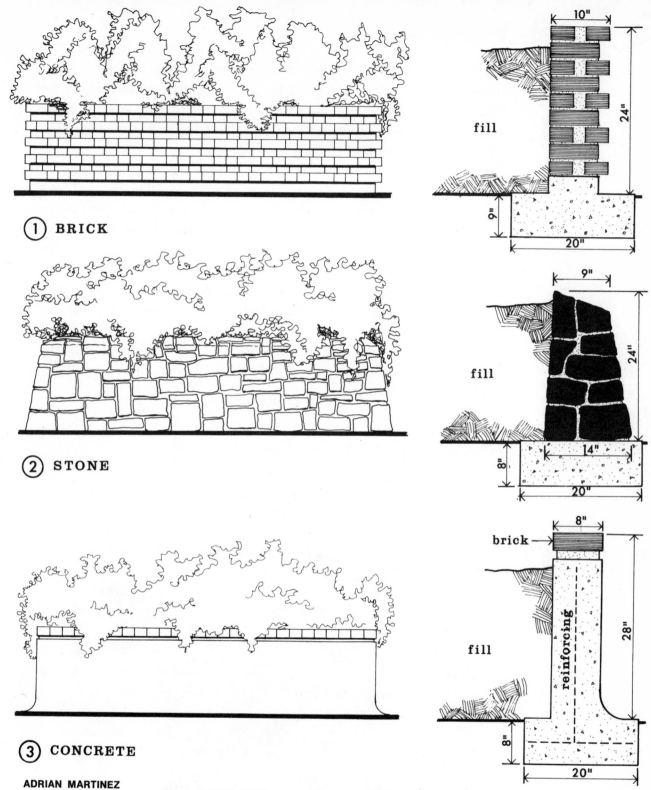

10"

24"

fill

9"

20"

① **BRICK**

9"

fill

24"

14"

8"

20"

② **STONE**

8"

brick

28"

reinforcing

fill

8"

20"

③ **CONCRETE**

ADRIAN MARTINEZ

Permanent Planters

sure the brick is evenly placed. When the wall has reached the desired height, trim it with a cap of concrete. Raised planters of this type can be used against a fence as entranceway highlights, or as retaining walls around the edges of patios, terraces, or walks. Circular and free-form designs can be built around trees or posts.

Some planters are permanent—that is, they are made for a specific area and are never moved. These may be wooden planters—generally the best—or a more elaborate or costly planter may be concrete or even stone. Other planters of wood, sometimes referred to as modular units, are boxes of the same size and shape that can be used in integral patterns in the garden. These are smaller than permanent planters; a 24-by-24-inch size is frequently used and is light enough to be easily carried by two people.

The advantage of the modular planter is that if you get tired of one arrangement you can move the boxes around to create a totally different garden. Whether a permanent wood planter or modular in design, the boxes are made in the same way and the drawings will help you to choose a satisfactory one for your garden.

107. This handsome planter is simple and elegant, an asset in any garden plan. (*Photo courtesy McGuire Furniture Company*)

11. Other Garden Structures

There are an infinite number of other garden shelters that the part-time handyman-gardener can make. This chapter is a catchall for these structures but by no means is a complete rundown of the many things that can be made for the outdoors. Here we look at the more popular items such as birdhouses, garden shelters (a wide variety of enclosures), lath houses, work centers, cold frames, and so forth.

Any of these items are easy to make or can be more difficult if you want elaborate designs. The beginner should stick to the simple things and later move on to other designs.

Wood and nails, hammer and saw, are again the basic tools you'll need, and your imagination.

BIRDHOUSES AND FEEDERS

Bringing the birds into your garden may horrify some people (those with fruit trees), but for most people birds are desirable. They are pretty, interesting, and above all they help keep down the harmful insect population. Normally, you will have some birds on the property but if you want to attract different species there are some things you can do. Build birdhouses for them and supply them with food over the winter. You will need a feeder for them; you can buy commercial birdhouses and feeders, of course, but the nicest ones are those you make yourself.

A house for birds can be almost any shape or size, but always should be above the ground. Certain birds have preferences for particular dwellings but most will come to almost any type of birdhouse. The interior need not be large, an 8-by-8-inch space is fine, but the size of the door

108. This service area is 1-by-4-inch tongue-and-groove cedar, horizontal 1-by-2-inch slats capped by 2 by 4s with a frame of 4-by-4-inch posts. The box holds two garbage cans; lids are 1-by-2-inch slats in a 2-by-2-inch frame. (*Photo courtesy Western Wood Products*)

(or opening) will of course vary for different birds. Wrens prefer a 1-to-2-inch circular opening and a 2-to-3-inch opening is adequate for most birds. Some houses should be open, others enclosed, and this again depends on the bird. Bluebirds, flickers, chickadees, tree swallows, and wrens will prefer an enclosed house; robins and barn swallows want an open house.

For the birdhouse use 1-inch boards or exterior ¾-inch plywood. Be sure the birdhouse is securely fastened to the pole. The pole itself should be embedded at least 8 to 10 inches deep in concrete.

Bird feeders can be merely shelves on a pole or attached to window ledges, again above ground level so cats and squirrels can't get the upper hand. You can use a piece of board on the top—sort of a roof—for weather protection—and glass-in the sides if you like; this will enable you to see when the food is gone.

GARDEN SHELTERS

These structures can be of various designs, some used for storing tools, others for shade areas, or a shelter can even be a gazebo. Sun traps are another idea—a partially open structure where you can sit in the sun; and pergolas are generally defined as arbors or trellises—a walk shaded by plants with the structure made of wood strips or branches or lathing.

COLD FRAMES

These look like windows on a box on the ground and while they may not be attractive they certainly are useful for gardeners. You can start seeds, store woody plants, winter over bulbs, and do dozens of other gardening necessities in a cold frame.

The unit is simply four walls—2-by-12-inch boards anchored in soil to a depth of 2 inches with a slightly sloped roof; the roof is window sash or plastic or glass in a wood frame. The smallest practical size is 2 by 4 feet but 4 by 6 feet is much better because commercial glass sash comes in these sizes.

Build the cold frame of resistant wood such as redwood or cedar. Put drainage at the bottom of the cold frame for best results. As mentioned, use glass or plastic for the frames and 2-by-2-inch corner posts. Use a gravel bed at the bottom—about 2 inches—or plastic coverings.

109. Dramatic and graceful, a garden shelter of redwood is the focal point of this garden. (*Photo courtesy California Redwood Association*)

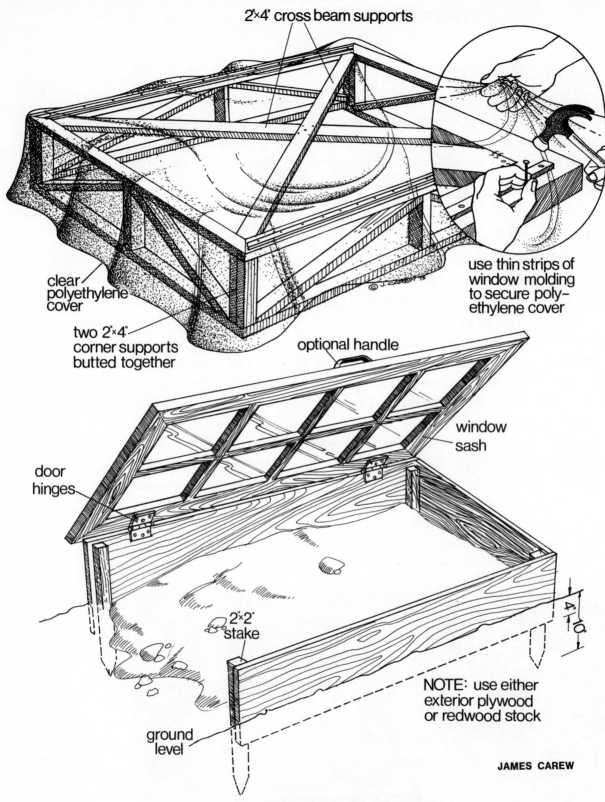

2×4' cross beam supports

use thin strips of window molding to secure poly- ethylene cover

clear polyethylene cover

two 2"×4" corner supports butted together

optional handle

window sash

door hinges

2×2" stake

4" 10"

ground level

NOTE: use either exterior plywood or redwood stock

JAMES CAREW

Cold Frame

WORK CENTERS

Work centers—potting tables, storage sheds—are a convenience and almost a necessity for the good gardener. Here you can keep tools and supplies together and if you work in the yard a lot you know how important it is to have everything in one place. It saves futile searching for tools, as well as time.

You might also want a small potting table with soil, mulches, and pots in the lower shelves. Bins and racks can be built into the potting table to store bulbs and tubers, for instance.

Locate the work center near the house and yard but do not allow it to become an obstruction in the garden. Behind a garage, in a service area, or along a back fence are some suitable locations.

If you do a lot of gardening you will want a storage shed—ready-made metal types are available at suppliers. These units are usually 6 by 8 feet and in them you can store carpentry tools as well as garden tools. If you want to build your own storage shed—and I particularly like the homemade wooden ones because they are more aesthetically pleasing—you can certainly do it. Use 2-by-4-inch redwood and plywood sheets to make a suitable small storage area. Provide wide doors for mowers and wheelbarrows. Build the unit with plenty of shelf space and storage bins and it can act as a complete garden center.

110. This work center pit has shelves at waist height for easy plant puttering; it is also an attractive structure in the landscape. (*Photo by Ken Molino*)

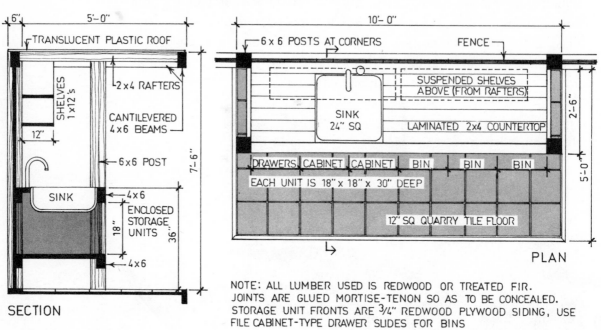

SECTION

6"   5'-0"

TRANSLUCENT PLASTIC ROOF

SHELVES 1×12's

2×4 RAFTERS

CANTILEVERED 4×6 BEAMS

12"

6×6 POST

7'-6"

SINK

4×6

ENCLOSED STORAGE UNITS

18"

36"

4×6

PLAN

10'-0"

6×6 POSTS AT CORNERS   FENCE

SUSPENDED SHELVES ABOVE (FROM RAFTERS)

SINK 24" SQ

LAMINATED 2×4 COUNTERTOP

2'-6"

5'-0"

DRAWERS | CABINET | CABINET | BIN | BIN | BIN

EACH UNIT IS 18" × 18" × 30" DEEP

12" SQ QUARRY TILE FLOOR

NOTE: ALL LUMBER USED IS REDWOOD OR TREATED FIR.
JOINTS ARE GLUED MORTISE-TENON SO AS TO BE CONCEALED.
STORAGE UNIT FRONTS ARE 3/4" REDWOOD PLYWOOD SIDING, USE
FILE CABINET-TYPE DRAWER SLIDES FOR BINS

Garden Work Center

design/drawing: Adrián Martinez

111. A garden work center behind the wooden frame is convenience plus. The cost is minimal and construction simple. (*Photo courtesy California Redwood Association*)

112. A barbecue pit made from concrete block and a suitable seating arrangement make this an ideal place to have dinner. (*Photo courtesy National Concrete Masonry Association*)

TRELLISWORK

If you have seen the old-fashioned arbor in a garden you have seen an effective example of trelliswork. Trellis structures are made of pieces of lath (1⅝ inches wide) crisscrossed one on the other in diamond or rectangular patterns. They are used for walls and fences for climbing plants and also for arbors where you usually see old-fashioned roses growing.

Making trellis structures is easy. Posts are put in place as for fence building and laths are nailed in place; it takes more patience than skill. The placement of posts will depend on the structure built—fence, trellis, lath house.

Lath is available in redwood or cedar in bundles of 50 or 100 pieces depending on the length, either 6 or 8 feet long. For most standing trellises in the garden, lath is satisfactory. For more substantial structures against a house wall for decoration, for example, use 1-by-20-inch lumber; more expensive but better looking.

SPECIAL OFFER FOR BOOK CLUB MEMBERS

Save $10 on these versatile Stellar 7 X 35 Binoculars

They're ideal all-purpose binoculars — good for a wide range of outdoor activities from football games to bird watching.

Look at these features:

☐ **Fully <u>coated optics.</u>** Both lenses and prisms are coated to give them maximum light-gathering power and to insure bright, clear, sharp images.

☐ **<u>Quick, accurate focusing</u>.** A right-eye adjustment compensates for differences in vision of the two eyes. A center focusing wheel permits fast adjustment.

☐ **<u>Magnification</u>.** "7 X" refers to the magnifying power of the binoculars. It means an object 700 feet away will appear to be only 100 feet away. "35" refers to the diameter in millimeters of the objective lenses, which determines the amount of light admitted. The larger the lenses, the greater the amount of light and the later in the evening you can use the binoculars.

☐ **<u>Field of View.</u>** The Stellar Binoculars provide a 393-foot field of view at 1000 yards.

☐ **<u>Weight.</u>** 21½ ounces.

The binoculars come in a soft vinyl case with carrying strap. You also get a shoulder strap and four lens covers.

Suggested Retail Price $49.95. Your Club Price only

$39⁹⁵

plus delivery and handling

Stellar 7 X 35 Binoculars are fully guaranteed against any defects in workmanship.

TO GET YOUR BINOCULARS, JUST SEND YOUR ORDER TO: BOOK CLUB P.O. BOX 2044, LATHAM, N.Y. 12111

Ask for STELLAR BINOCULARS, NO. 7000, and enclose your check or money order for $39.95 plus $3.10 for delivery and handling and we'll send you your binoculars right away.